FERDINAND FUELLER

Heart Without Frontiers

A True Story

Written in collaboration with Stella Gimenez.

The events I narrate in this book are classified as historical nonfiction. What you are about to read is my true story. Some names have been changed to protect people's privacy.

Everything in this book is factual - as alive for me today as ever, still fresh enough to share it with you now.

First edition

ISBN: 9781099652639

Cover art by Yulieth Genoy Puerto and Diego Carenzo
Editing by Joan Anne Nathan and David Brizer

This book was professionally typeset on Reedsy.
Find out more at reedsy.com

To Joe, my beloved brother

Contents

Acknowledgments

I want to give thanks to all the adverse circumstances and challenges that have crossed my path, even though any one of them could have ended my life! These obstacles have toughened my spirit and given me the resiliency and persistence to accomplish the significant achievements of my life.

If I had lived in a state of total comfort, without having to face the difficult and painful challenges I've been through, I would have become a mindless drone, a monotonous being unaware of the real values of life.

Above all, I give thanks to all the people who opened their hearts and their doors and offered me opportunities to continue to grow and evolve: my parents, my wife, my children, siblings, and all the great family without whom I would have been unable to keep improving my life.

I thank God, immensely, for inspiring me with a spirit capable of feeling His guidance. I have never doubted his presence; instead, I have always let myself flow, buoyed by the knowledge that He has created a meaningful, important purpose for my life.

There are so many others I wish to thank, but I would have to devote an entire book to express my boundless gratitude to them.

But I know that my gratitude will reach their hearts. To everyone who has been with me each step of the way, and to those who still support me: Thank you!

Introduction

I was born in a country that no longer exists: *"Yugoslavia"*.

I belong to the descendants of a monarchical dynasty that began in 1020 and became extinct in the 18th Century: *"The House of Habsburg"*.

My forebears were German. My DNA is German. As a boy, my classmates derided and humiliated me, calling me *"Nazi"* and punishing me severely and cruelly, although I have never discriminated against anyone because of their race or because of their religious or cultural background. My mother taught me these values.

I am a survivor. I survived myriad death threats: death threats I received before I was born, when I was born, and throughout the trajectory of my life.

According to the lore of my ancestors, my 'hawk', (*Habicht* in German) was seen guarding a castle's wall and so *"Habsburg"* became the name of this dynasty. Could it be that my mother had a hawk as a guardian angel, a hawk whose proud vigilance gave my mother courage and wisdom to save my just born life?

There were so many times I could have died. But I didn't. A spiritual force transcended the dangers that threatened my life. Today, in spite of all the hardship I have endured, I continue walking along the path that destiny has shaped for me.

My life has been an ongoing learning process. I strode the corridors of destiny with an open heart and a free mind. I learned to be tolerant of and to appreciate the differences of others, and to never surrender to the belief that at the same time, to flow driven by an indomitable instinct that has never surrendered to the belief that *'this won't be possible to achieve'.*

I have overcome each and every obstacle that barred my way - as though my determination to achieve a better life was inherited, an inborn expression of an indomitable spirit. Perhaps that somehow explains why my mother did not choose to abort. When I was a newborn she left me in the wilderness - but somehow I survived. This will to survive prevented me from succumbing to the atrocities of the war that raged for years in the Balkans.

I discovered something important about myself as I navigated the deadly storms of my life: I learned that I chose to live as a citizen of the world rather than as a nationalist or sectarian devotee of emblems or flags. I realized that my heart knows no frontiers. I love this.

I want to share my story with you for many reasons. One is to let the world know a widely unrecognized fact: the Germans too have suffered atrocious deaths, abhorrent tortures, and continuous rapes. *Germans* were considered, as an ethnic group, to have been essentially erased from former Yugoslavia - erased forever - during Tito's dictatorship. German homes were routinely confiscated. We lost what we possessed as a result of degrading, abusive behaviors from both the partisans and from those who supported the partisans' determination to eliminate *"people of German blood".* We also suffered the torments of concentration camps during Tito's time.

My mother's spirit, was a widespread umbrella, a precious and unceasing fountain of wisdom. I learned that there was no procedural manual for living a life of dignity and achievement.

Her words, like a bell, to this day, ring loud and clear, inspiring my journey:

> *"Follow your heart wherever you go. Have faith in your dreams. Behave with ethics and honor no matter what you do, big or small. Carry forward your life with an expanding spirit, with confidence, a desire to learn, and always keep moving to overcome your frustrations. Improve yourself at each step of the road. Always tolerate and respect the ideas of others without diluting or suppressing your own innermost and precious beliefs. Allow your heart to beat as though you lived in a world without frontiers. Embracing the sacred richness of our vast worldwide diversity."*

I once read a remarkable quotation from Martin Luther King. Jr. He said: "When we look at modern man, we have to face the fact...that modern man suffers from a kind of poverty of the spirit, which stands in glaring contrast to his scientific and technological abundance; We've learned to fly in the air like birds, we've learned to swim the seas like fish, and yet we haven't learned to walk the Earth as brothers and sisters..."

After so many thousands of years still it remains terribly difficult for us to develop a spirit of brotherhood, or a humanitarian spirit, in a world dominated by the raucous voices of greediness, separation, intolerance, and an incredible thirst to harm other living beings on our planet. We live on the precipice, almost overwhelmed by irrational destructive acts against life; we turn the other way, and pretend that our violence and narrow-mindedness have no consequences.

I grew up believing in my inner voice and I have evolved with it as my only guidepost in the face of chaos and misfortune.

This is my story.

Ferdinand Fueller
Maryland
July, 2019

"All human beings are born free and equal in dignity and rights. They are endowed with reason and conscience and should act towards one another in a spirit of brotherhood."

(Article 1 of the <u>Universal Declaration of Human Rights</u>)

"Humanity should be our race. Love should be our religion."

Unknown

1

The Birth of the Hawk Spirit

*"If you want to fly you have to give up
the things that weigh you down."*

Toni Morrison - "Song of Solomon"

I agree! When we need to fly we need metaphorical wings. We need to let go of all those things that prevent us from soaring along our evolutionary flight path.

The things I used to know and got so very accustomed to: all there was to create *a 'comfort zone'* which was soothing in the short term but spiritually deadly in the long run. Remain in a benighted comfort zone long enough and retrograde evolution - *'de-evolution'* - was guaranteed.

To this day I do not know if I had been born with his indwelling spirit of forward movement or if I had sucked it up from the long forced marches along the road of frustrations. Either way, I never stopped hoping that one day I would reach the life of my most profound dreams. What I do know is that I have lived with my hands open not only to give but also to receive and to let go of finished business in my life.

When she wasn't working on her parent's farm, my mother and my two older brothers lived in a small village in Yugoslavia. Her name was Maria in German - *Marizi* in Slavish. During her youth, they called her *'the bird of light'.* She did everything fast and efficiently, flying, with a smile and a heavenly light in her eyes that brought peace to everyone she knew. Her gait was avian, with the lightness of purposeful flight. She always knew what she had to do, going about her tasks with the same fervent devotion she gave to daily prayers and Catholic mass. She was the spirit piloting her family ship against all storms, harvesting even more inner strength in times of calm. It was the year 1941. She lived with my elder siblings in former Yugoslavia. She was young, strong and beautiful. She was devoted to the Holy Spirit and had an unshakeable faith in God. No matter what happened, her indomitable spirit kept her afloat, even during the worst of times.

My mother worked on her parents' farm, dividing her time between their home in the town and the farming duties. 95% of the ethnic Germans were small farmers; my mother and her Yugoslavian Germanic ancestors were no exception. They had been very well organized, creating the agricultural associations that contributed positively to the economic life of Yugoslavia, especially in the years following the *Great Depression.* By 1941, a large majority of the German ethnic families belonged to these associations, empowering them to minimize the consequences of the economic crisis during these times of great world famine.

A certain level of intolerance toward the ethnic Germans began to grow during those years. Perhaps the intolerant and bigoted found the Germans' level of well being, organization, and productivity (for the nation as a whole) intolerable. The lives of ethnic Germans who lived or who had even been born in Yugoslavia were not secure, compared to the lives of other young men of war age.

There were too many moments when the abominations against innocent civilians were inconceivable. The ethnic persecution had begun - not yet massively, but cruelly and in covert and clandestine ways. The desire to erode the lives of those considered to be of 'German blood' began with attacks, with repeated rapes on women and girls. The intended extermination: extermination through horror and terror. Russians and Tito's partisans united with resentful locals against ethnic Germans to create what they called 'the rape tour,' carried out at any time of day, but especially at night. Many of the perpetrators, their heads covered with hoods, would invade the homes of women and girls whose brothers and husbands had been sent off to war. Not infrequently, they arrived drunk, anaesthetized to any feelings of guilt for their aberrant acts. In many cases, they achieved their goal of violently raped, slaughter and murder.

It was 1941. Christmas was approaching and the village was getting dressed for the celebration. My mother wanted us to feel the joy of this celebration. With little money but great ingenuity, she managed to decorate our home. She lived alone with her two children; my father had to flee to Bosnia to escape the ruthless partisans of Tito, who were on a mission to hunt down and kill him and any others considered to be enemies of their political ideas.

As part of their strategy to instill terror in the community, and to manifest their hatred of anyone considered of 'German blood,' Tito's partisans mercilessly applied their strategy of extermination: the elimination of Germans who lived in the Yugoslavian territory *by the constant physical and emotional rape of women and girls.*

There was nothing my mother could do to prevent the constant acts of rape by Tito's partisans. They came into the house, their heads hooded to avoid being recognized while repeatedly abusing my mother. My mother didn't dare to oppose them, fearing for the life of her children. My mother was a martyr who had to pretend that nothing horrendous was destroying her life.

These nightmare events are burned permanently into my brain.

One Christmas night when my mother was serving dinner and saying a Christmas prayer, one of the partisans sauntered into the house and raped her. That was the night I was conceived, a bastard son of an unknown biological father. The violence violation nauseated her and she began to and vomit all the time. Her inner strength was remarkable, heaven-sent. Unconsciously, she couldn't bear the idea of giving life to a child fathered by one of those Tito's partisans.

One afternoon she went to her parents' farm. She passed near the hut of a sorceress she knew superficially, a woman with whom she had exchanged occasional cordial greetings. My mother began to vomit until she fell on her knees, crying inconsolably. Suddenly she heard the voice of the sorceress. *"You have a child in your womb, and he is not just any child."* To which my mother replied, *"Thank you, but I am a woman of the Catholic faith, and I do not believe in oracles or superstitions . . ."* The sorceress interrupted her. *"It does not matter if you believe me or not, it is the truth."* Looking at the sky and raising her arms she added, *" . . . when the child is born a hawk will fly over you. That will be the signal that will tell you that he will come close to death many times but he will not die."* My mother got up and ran to the house to go to bed, exhausted, sobbing and broken.

After her encounter with the sorceress, my mother started

having unusual dreams. She vividly saw herself flying out of her body while she slept, knowing full well that the human body doesn't fly. She recalled her dreams when she woke up. My mother also thought that she started seeing a hawk flying once in a while and believed that perhaps the old woman had triggered these ideas and she started praying more often.

Two months had passed since she learned of her pregnancy and my mother ran desperately to the church to confess to the priest what she needed to do. She begged him for permission to abort me. The priest, full of compassion and understanding her feelings, replied that the Catholic Church considers abortion a crime because the unborn child is already a creature of God, a living human being with spirit and consciousness.

My mother left the church feeling helpless. She asked God to take me with Him; the child she had in her womb had been conceived by an unworthy man whom she did not even know, a man who had raped her and many other women repeatedly. She asked God for forgiveness for the disgust she felt towards those violations and toward the baby in her womb created by an act of violation. One of her relatives had self-inflicted an abortion and died after a severe infection.

The nine months went by - the passage of time is irrepressible - and my mother had not gained much weight because she worked hard at home and on the farm and did not eat very well. She was depressed and perhaps not eating in order to terminate the pregnancy.

But on the mild morning of September 27, 1942, as she was collecting hay on the farm her labor contractions began. She ran to the barn, but her water broke on the way. With all her strength she grasped the thick branch of an oak tree and so, semi-sitting and semi-standing, inhaling and exhaling, panting and crying, she allowed me passage through her female channels and so I was born. I gently slid on to the hay that had fallen from her hands when the contractions began. I cried. We both cried. She took the knife she had to winnow the grass and cut the umbilical cord; then, she stood up and with her remaining strength, ran to the farmhouse and abandoned me in the field, left to my fate.

She stumbled just before reaching the house. Weeping and sweating, shaking like a leaf in the wind, she heard a sound in the sky. She looked up and saw a hawk circling over the place where she had left me. A burst of adrenaline enabled her to get up and run back to my side. She wrapped me in her apron, lifted me, hugged me, and kissed me, wetting my face with her tears and asking me and God for forgiveness. The sorceress watched all this from her doorway.

My mother raised me with infinite love. She protected me and my older siblings from the horrid events that were taking place more and more frequently each day in our town in Yugoslavia. The same town where the partisans had been expropriated the ethnic Germans' belongings in order to remove all evidence that those Germans had ever lived or been born in Yugoslavia.

She took precautions. looking for good places to hide all our birth certificates and other important documents identifying us as owners of the familial properties. Properties that had been earned legitimately through years of hard work and devotion to our farms. Our ethnic Germanic ancestors had settled in Yugoslavia some three hundred years ago. Those times of peace and progress through sacrifice starting eroding from the continual onslaught of hatred, violence, and rape.

2

The Unthinkable

The End of our Yugoslavia

Before he left office, American President George W Bush said:
"Genocide was committed...during Yugoslavia."

The horror that followed the unthinkable times of hatred and murder against the ethnic German was growing in the darkness. The well organized Germanic-Yugoslavian culture in Yugoslavia, based on education and the community's commitment to ethical behavior and hard work in the field, was repugnant to Tito's followers. At the end of the First World War, and after the disappearance of the Austro-Hungarian Empire, the ethnic Germans were reassigned to the new successor states of the Habsburg Empire: the Kingdom of the Serbs, Croats, and Slovenes (Yugoslavia), Romania and Hungary.

By the early 1920s, some 500,000 German speakers lived were the largest minority in Yugoslavia (compared to the Hungarian and Albanian minorities.) The largest group of Germans were concentrated in the area of the Danube plain. Although a minority, the ethnic Germans had achieved significant cultural and economic organization in Yugoslavia between World War I and World War II.

After World War II, to their great misfortune, the German ethnic group in Yugoslavia was considered part of Nazi Germany and as the *bourgeois descendants of the imperialists*. None of these fatuous connections helped the innocent people labeled as those of the 'German blood.'

The disappearance of the Austro-Hungarian Empire inspired a new consciousness of identity among the ethnic Germans of Yugoslavia; the extinction of the Habsburgs was directly related to the idea of a dynastic descent belonging to *German culture*.

After the Paris Peace Conference, coinciding with a stable Yugoslavia in the early 1920s, the creation of a German ethnic movement was promoted to strengthen its German identity. Lectures and cultural activities focused on the values and achievements of German culture; such as language, art, music, philosophy, literature, and science.

Because the majority of the members of the German minority were small farmers, they created agricultural associations that contributed positively to the life of Yugoslavia, especially in the years following the "Great Depression." By 1941, a large majority of the German ethnic families belonged to these associations and managed to alleviate the problems of an economic crisis that everyone suffered during times of great world famine. But during World War II and immediately following the post-war period, violent attacks spurred on by ideological differences and ethnic intolerance continued with renewed force. The distinction between 'civilians' and 'combatants' disappeared, resulting in terrible massacres against all groups, including the innocents. The German ethnic groups of Yugoslavia became the first and main target of extermination. Slovenian Germans who could not escape in time were expelled; the ethnic Germans of Batschka and Banat were less fortunate.

The persecution of the German minority began with the settlements of the Red Army and continued with the partisans. As a result of the abominable quest for extermination, German minority women and girls were victims of indiscriminate violations by occupation forces.

There is no doubt that World War II had constituted one of the most egregious horrors against humanity; yet the survivors were not prepared for the terrible atrocities that many of them would receive following the end of that war. Millions of ethnic Germans from Eastern Europe were either horribly massacred or expelled from their lands in former Yugoslavia. Such was the case with my family.

The collective trauma of these barbaric attacks and injuries received at all physical and psychological levels were unimaginable and largely unrecorded: it is difficult to find reliable information regarding the terrifying genocidal attacks committed against the ethnic Germans.

It is believed that the annihilation and forced removal of ethnic Germans was simply hidden because people of Germanic blood were during the Post-World War II period were considered for Nazis, responsible for the massacres and horrors of the Holocaust that led to in the extermination of millions of Jews (among others) by the Nazi regime.

We have survived the persecutions and massacres carried out against the Germans who lived in Yugoslavia. Yugoslavia had been my country of birth. Yet we clung toward a humanitarian spirit, an evolving spirit, in order to contain and if possible dispel resentment and smoldering hatred towards those responsible for the extermination of so many innocent lives and for the loss of our belongings in our Yugoslavia.

The Yugoslavia that came after the Second World War was the center of multiple conflicts: *resistance, class war, ethnic violence, criminal networks,* and *personal issues at the local level.*

The sheer number of horrendous deaths that occurred during the post-war period qualified as genocide. It is estimated of more than 1.2 million people was killed, among whom almost 600,000 were innocent civilians.

The murders had increased in Yugoslavia at the end of the war without justified political purposes. The brutal behavior following World War II had been fueled by post-war resentment; what was paramount in Yugoslavia was the fear that the allied forces would be supported by the non-communist armed groups. The communist authorities, who were independent of the Soviet Union, planned to annihilate their national opponents to strengthen and protect the Tito's new regime. In this way, the new regimen directly supported actions in the massacres, unlike other countries where reprisals against opponents were not supported by the state.

Communist leader Josip Broz ("Tito") quickly consolidated his power of extermination strategies that began when the war was in its final stage.

Post-war violence was evident in the killing of civilians in order to dismantle by total cruelty the local anti-party forces, including the fascist and the realist forces. Along with this plan came the forced expulsion of the non-Slavic populations (like the German and Hungarian ethnic communities.) This led to more atrocity and deaths, and the ruthless torture of more than 150,000 people between 1945 and 1948.

Fleeing from the imminent dangers that were about to threaten their lives, before Zagreb fell under the power of the partisans, those opposed to Tito's regime began their escape to the north of Austria with the hope that they could surrender to the British forces. This never happened. Some of those who crossed into Austria at Bleiberg on May 15, 1945, did not receive the support of the English to accept surrender. The tragic result of that trip was that the English handed them over to the partisans and many were horribly murdered. Evidence has been found that almost all the crimes against them occurred after the Ustaše and the Slovenian forces were massacred by the partisans when they were handed over to them as they crossed the border. This was followed by a considerable number of killings of prisoners of war and civilians on the way to Maribor and after reaching the concentration camps.

Many of the large-scale massacres involved throwing people off of the mountains; mass graves containing the bodily remains of victims who died during the journey were found, as well. Nobody had food or water. All had been stripped of their belongings and forced to make long marches.

Those who lost their strength were shot. The deaths occurred because of the aberrant whim of the partisans, who took sadistic pleasure in killing anyone, at any time. Many victims were murdered after having been tortured or raped.

Already in Maribor, the groups were separated into civilians, soldiers of rank, and others, according to their level of leadership. Those considered 'less guilty' were sent to concentration camps throughout the country. Those who were judged as culprits were massacred and buried in common graves.

Tito gave orders that the Ustaše were not to be killed. He wanted them to be taken to the concentration camps to personally punish the most culpable and to apply the most severe legal actions. Nonetheless the murders continued. Those who were not lucky enough to be released were relocated to concentration camps scattered throughout the country and underwent terrible tortures; many were killed. The murders continued.

Those considered ethnic Germans, along with the Hungarians, suffered terrible deaths at the end of the Second World War.

The atrocities and suffering were unimaginable. The partisans inflicted terrible damage on the many who fell into their hands. The partisans' thirst for diabolical torture and infllicting enormous suffering was unquenchable. Groups of Germans and Hungarians were killed *en masse.* The largest communities had concentrated in the northeastern and central northern parts of Yugoslavia. Some had grouped into districts located in towns such as Novi Sad Osijek.

During these persecutions and massacres, almost a quarter million Germans managed to be evacuated. Even when the policy was one of expulsion and expropriation of the property of all Germans, many civilians were massacred in their homes, on their farms and in the concentration camps. Again, a major weapon of extermination had been to repeatedly rape women and girls until they died or had their children.

It was in November, 1944 when the Communist-led Anti-Fascist Popular Liberation Council of Yugoslavia appropriated all the assets of the Germans living there. I was two years old, managing as well as we could with our hawk-like mother at the helm. Our father was still away. The partisans burned down the Courthouse and the Church to get rid of all the documents in town. This erased all testimonies of the Germans who had lived or had been born there.

Tito said those of 'German blood' who lived here were all traitors to his regime. The Communist leadership made clear its intention to expel the ethnic Germans, who were seen as traitors one and all.

It is estimated that some 2,000 ethnic German intellectuals and leaders who lived in the northwestern parts were attacked and massacred by the partisans in 1944. More than 10,000 died in cold blood and in terribly ruthless ways; among them included more than 12,000 people who had been deported to Soviet concentration camps. Not only did the partisans commit abominable bloody acts, there were also locals who took advantage of the flood of cold blood to release their hatred towards those called 'The Germans.'

Their violation of human rights constituted a genocide that lasted for more than four years (between 1944 and 1948). Among the people of Yugoslavia who lost all their assets and ended up in concentration camps were hundreds of thousands of children, women and men who died after horrendous tortures, constant rape, hunger, diseases, and other strategies of extermination (such as adding ground glass to the food given to the refugees so that they would die of internal hemorrhage). Between 1945 and 1948 the plan was *"to cause the death of as many people as possible."*

After the years 1948 and 1950 the ethnic Germans were forbidden on pain of death to return to their villages; if they appeared in the cities, they were forced to emigrate. It is estimated that the genocide perpetrated against ethnic Germans and Hungarians after the Second World War involved the extermination of 70,000 people.

My not biological father was serving in a branch of the Yugoslav army known as the Prince Eugene Regiment. He was not at home when my mother was repeatedly raped by partisans. I imagine that if my mother's husband would have been at home, they would have killed him and then raped my mother anyway. From now on, I will refer to my not biological father Ferdinand as 'my father' because he loved me as he did the rest of my siblings.

At the time of my birth, my mother and father already had two children. I became number three. I am still amazed whenever I think about the strong devotion our mother gave not only to her children, but also supporting her husband with the trauma he experienced in the war which lead him to alcohol. Perhaps her wise compassion helped him to eventually get back to himself and helped her to raise her children with peace and harmony.

My mother led us down a path of goodness. Goodness of heart, goodness of spirit, goodness of soul. We were always guided by her wisdom, understanding, and compassion. She told us of a priest who had taught her: *"Self-control is the strength. Right thought is mastery. Calmness is power."*

My siblings and I were fortunate to have been inspired by her unconditional love. She never expressed resentment about the dreadful abuse we had to endure. My mother's victimization was probably the worst of all; she was raped several times a day and perhaps one day she would not resist any longer and just die. Rapes committed on women and girls, even little girls, were actually an ancillary weapon of extermination during the war. The terrible panic and emotional trauma were additional forms of dominance over enemy ethnic groups.

For some, the end of World War II marked the beginning of one of the worst periods of their lives.

My family were survivors of the persecutions aimed at the ethnic Germans, specifically the Danube Swabians in Yugoslavia at the end of the war. We were removed from our homes and forced to leave our properties to the partisans, who took control of our country right after the Russian troops marched into our towns.

The partisans looted everyone's businesses. Everything was taken from us. Women and girls in a panic had to find safe places to hide each night to avoid being raped by Russian soldiers or supporters. All ethnic Germans were forced to work in the fields and to give up the life they used to live before the Second World War. Most German men, no matter their age, were hauled out from their homes and terribly mistreated, beaten and tortured. Some were brutally killed, their lifeless bodies left in the streets to create even more horror in those who saw them die. They ground the flesh of other murder victims, cooked it and gave it as food to the starving people who lived in the concentration camps. There were many other atrocities too. Their bodies of people were cut in half and hung in the door-ways of their homes, further demonstrated horrendous things that the partisans were capable of doing against civilians and opponents of the Tito regime.

In some camps, the partisans would bring people to the work-places and then take them back late in the day. They counted how many they were and when their numbers were less than the day before, they forced the prisoners to stand still in the cold until midnight. If the children tried to get back to their mothers while they were working in the camps, the partisans beat them very hard.

My parents told me that one of the camps held more than 8,000 people. Life there made it almost impossible to be hopeful and hold on to life. They came to check up on everyone, and people who were in good physical condition would be forced to labor camp; the rest, such as the sick, elderly and disabled, mothers with small children, were sent to extermination camps like Gakovo, Krushevlje, and Ridjica, where several thousand starved to death. All lived near starvation, enduring beatings, rape, broken bones and broken backs, and sleep deprivation.

We had to watch the murders and suffered constant panic, not knowing what would be the worst or who would die next. Camps like Gakowa were sites of extermination and other dreadful mistreatment.

At the end of the WWII, the Soviet troops arrested hundreds of thousands of civilians of German ethnicity in Eastern European countries. These people had been transferred to internment camps. Most of the imprisoned died; those who survived existed under unimaginable misery. Words cannot express the level of suffering, coercion, violence, and deep emotional trauma that people endured. We all went to the 'forced removal events' to fulfill the desires of Tito and his partisans to proceed with 'the ethnic cleansing; mass murder, torture, and genocide. Those who didn't die experienced unmitigated sadistic behavior and cruelty.

By the end of WWII, over fifteen thousand ethnic German civilians had been deported, had their properties expropriated by the partisans, and about two million died. Approximately 55.000 ethnic Germans were forced to work in the labor camps died there or were murdered in atrocious circumstances.

We were among the blessed few who managed in 1944 to flee to Austria.

The uprooting and destruction was unimaginable and indescribable. After all the horror and misery had been indelibly branded in our memories, healing was only possible by nurturing ourselves with forgiveness - not ever allowing any resentment to fester in our minds or spirits.

Many never knew and today still don't know that the ethnic Germans were deported, killed, and enslaved. Children were placed in orphanages. The physical suffering was not compatible with life. Beyond that, the psychological trauma left very deep and incurable wounds. Anyone with German blood was doomed: beaten, mutilated, turned out of doors, or otherwise tortured, The ethnic Germans existed with insufficient food and medicine, under miserably inadequate sanitation, which led to infections and death.

Life in the concentration camps was the ultimate degradation. One waited to be killed to end the horrifying, never-ending situations.

There are very few sources in English that document the true stories of ethnic German civilians, although more recently some testimonies have come to light. Stories about the forced expulsion of people of 'German blood' were overlooked and ignored; perhaps the Germans deserved their horrifying punishment since many believed they had been directly associated with the atrocities committed by the Nazis during World War II.

However, historical comparisons and enumerations of the massive human toll can only be understood as atrocities against innocent civilians. The stories of survivors, like those from my own family, relatives, and friends, are testimonies of the harmful consequences of violent forced removal.

Tito's coldly-calculated rationale was that the more cruelty the Axis inflicted on ordinary Yugoslavs, the greater the numbers who would join the partisans' crusade to liberate Yugoslavia. Someone who survived time in a Nazi concentration camp fell into the clutches of the genocides led by Tito, the so-called 'ONZa.' Tito said that *"... if the Gestapo had ravaged the bodies, the ONZa had raped the soul of the innocents."*

The dreadful occupation of Yugoslavia between 1941 - 1945 was textbook genocide, genocide that took the lives of over 1.8 million people. The mass murders were committed by the partisans' purges for political and ethnic reasons.

But there were other 'actors' behind the scenes of Tito's operations. There were Agreements between allied forces that weighed heavily on the conscience of Great Britain and the United States. The intolerable conditions were *"carried out under the auspices, and with the full approbation of the international community."* Stalin wanted to expel the Germans, while the United States and Great Britain hoped to reduce the bloody expulsions and attacks of revenge, thereby establishing a process of eviction that would be more peaceful and moderate. As Soviet forces in the east brutally expelled Germans, the Allies sought through the Potsdam Agreement to make the forced removals more humanitarian.

The 'orderly transfer' of the German population was explicitly authorized in the Potsdam Agreement, resulting in the extermination of 12 million ethnic Germans from parts of central and eastern Europe. The Yalta agreement spoke of 'Reparations in kind' that served as punitive measures for war crimes committed by the Nazis. When I shared our stories elsewhere, people who didn't know what really happened to the ethnic Germans assumed that my story told of a relatively isolated experience. Others thought that what had happened to ethnic Germans was retribution for the Nazi atrocities of World War II. In the aftermath of the war, Soviet troops and partisan forces under the leadership of Joseph Stalin and Marshal Tito justified the brutal punishment and murder of civilians and the exclusion of ethnic Germans from Soviet-occupied areas.

This forced removal of ethnic Germans is a piece of history that is often left out of the narratives of human cruelty, perhaps because those who were aware of these massacres might have thought of them as deserved, justifying brutality because of brutality. Exploiting the victims' ethnic connection to those who committed the crimes does not absolve the victimizers.

3

Growing Up as Slaves

*"You can chain me, you can torture me, you can even destroy
this body, but you will never imprison my mind."*

Mahatma Gandhi

I was only two years old when my family fled to save our lives in
October and November, 1944. The Soviets, the British, and even
the United States were bombing innocent civilians like us while
we were escaping in horse-drawn carts. Hundreds of civilians
were killed by the bombs. Of the more than 300 families fleeing,
less than half of them made it to Graz, Austria.

Our family was one of the lucky ones. We survived those
attacks when we fled from the bloody murders of the partisans.
We left at dawn. The Sun had not yet come out. Winter was
approaching as we were expelled to our fate in exile. Escape
meant crossing a border that would open the door to a more
hopeful life. But we were going to arrive, if we did arrive, with
empty hands and frozen hearts.

We were traveling by horse and wagon in a convoy as they

attacked us. Approximately three hundred families were fleeing. Less than half of these families made it to Graz, Austria. We were one of the lucky ones who had not died during those attacks. When they managed to stop us, the partisans searched the wagons for documents they needed to justify the theft of our property. My mother had heard about the search for these documents so she sewed them into a feather blanket, placing me on top of the heap to cover them up. She later said that it was fortunate that I was crying so loudly, because they were loathe to pick up a screaming child. The documents she had hidden inside the blanket were never found. My mother's siblings were not as fortunate; they didn't protect their documents. The partisans confiscated all of them and they lost their right to what they already owned at the time.

It took more than two months to get to Austria. We had to haul the wagon with only one horse because the other died on the way. When we arrived at the southern part of Austria, we were confined for the Winter in an Austrian concentration camp.

We all became enslaved, vulnerable, and defenseless against the aberrant treatment we received at the hands of the farmers. The despotism and tyranny of the farmer submerged our lives in hunger and fear.

Our mother taught us the invaluable secret of resilience in the face of hatred, scorn, and disgust. We were treated like filthy animals. Instead of 'being a man created of mud', as the Bible says, the farmers believed we had been made from evil, and from livestock dung.

In spite of those terrible living conditions, a strong spirit of survival was growing in us, and the determination to obtain a better life one day remained our credo. Our credo kept us alive.

In the Spring of 1945, we were assigned to stay with an Austrian farmer. There, five of us lived in two rooms of no larger than 10' by 10'. We had no bathroom, no kitchen, no sinks, and no running water. The story gets worse. We were not allowed to use the outhouse that the Austrian farm family was using; we had to use a pot when we had to do our business. We used a big galvanized tub to take a bath. My mother said that I was always crying because I was hungry and my stomach was probably hurting. There wasn't any food. Sometimes she would get a loaf of bread as black as a lump of coal which she embedded with water and sprinkled with some sugar or salt to provide us with something to relieve the hunger pangs.

About five months later, on May 5, 1945, later my mother gave birth to my sister Teresia, whom we used to call 'Resi.' A year later, on November 17, 1946, my other sister Elisabeth was born. We named her 'Lisi.' There were five children to feed in times without food or shelter.

My oldest brother, who was born in 1935, had to work on another farm. He was too old to attend school; during the war he had missed his chance. So he never went to school. My brother was far from the love of our family, but the farmer and his wife who kept him, and treated him like their own son: they didn't have any children. He used to visit us during the weekends and gave my mother the money he had earned during the week.

When I was three years old, my 'Tante' Anna, as we used to call our Aunt Anna, came to visit us from Linz. She was working at a cheese factory. She was not married and had children at the time; she would bring us cheese from her work. One day Tante Anna was visiting. Somehow I managed to go out and when they noticed I was gone they looked for me everywhere. They went separate ways to find me. Tante Anna went to where there was a cow manure pit; she saw something moving under the manure crust. Something told her to put her hand in it and under it, and that was how she found me. She was screaming to her sister, my mother, to come to her just as she pulled me out. Both sisters thought that I was dead, when miraculously, I started vomiting manure liquid and began to breathe once again.

My mother used to take her children with her to a state forest, a one-hour walk from the farm where we stayed. We picked blueberries, raspberries, and mushrooms; foraging was allowed because the park belonged to the government. She would sell the leftovers so she could buy food for us. At first, we had to live with the Austrian family while my father worked for them. Sometime later, one year perhaps, he was working at the United States Army base in Salzburg; his job was to bag up wheat that was in salt mines for the German military.

When I was five years old, my mother handed me a burlap bag, picked me up and put me through the window, setting me down on the ground. She told me to go where the cows were to gather grass and put it in the bag. It was nighttime, and I was terrified. We found out later that she made soup from the grass I gathered to keep us alive. If the farmers had noticed, it would have been terrible for our family. We were not allowed not even to lift the dried branches that had fallen from the trees. Those already dead branches would have kept us warm in those tiny bedrooms.

Since my mother was a devout Catholic, we had to go with her to church. There, we were not allowed to sit on the bench even if it was unoccupied. Every time we went to church we had to stand in the back - stand there until we had to kneel on the cold stone floor. The faith of my mother kept her straight and standing with the dignity of a Spartan woman. Seeing my courageous mother, who never complained or showed any pain, gave me the courage to concentrate more on the sermon of the

Mass than on the humiliation that we constantly had to endure.

We were living as slaves of the Austrian farmers. Our own farms, and the farms of our families, as well as those of other Yugoslavs considered to be Germanic ethnicity, were expropriated by the partisans of the dictator Tito.

A year later, when I was six, a mean Austrian boy who hated the refugees approached me. He pushed me off the dock and threw me into the water. I started to sink because I could not swim. If my brother Josef hadn't been there to save my life, I wouldn't be writing this now.

When I was seven years old, a cable broke on the bicycle handlebar. It almost caught off my right big toe - a terrible frightening sight, just barely hanging there. When I was in the waiting room to see the doctor, he was distraught because of all the blood that spurted on his floor. Angrily he called me 'damn refugee.' I think today how steely strong our spirits must have been to survive not only the scarcity of food, the awful living conditions and, above all, being constantly mistreated in the land we were born.

Since the onset of hatred toward those considered of German blood, living in Yugoslavia we had all suffered in so many ways: being forced to surrender our belongings; what we had to endure in the concentration camps; and later, the intolerance of many farmers who used us as their slaves and degraded us as human beings.

At eight, my cousin, a friend, and I saw through a window that our school principal and the priest were eating meat at our local guest house on a Friday evening - an evening when everyone is supposed to eat fish. Suddenly the priest saw us looking at them through the window. Monday morning, the priest said to me that I will go to hell if I said anything about them eating meat on

Friday. I replied, "I guess I will see you in hell." That Monday he made me kneel down on corn that was on a concrete floor. When he left the room, I climbed down a pear tree from the second floor and didn't dare go home: my parents wouldn't believe me. I stayed in the dark, and heard my parents and friends looking for me and calling my name out loud. I only went back home in the morning, and my mother told my father not to punish me when she saw the bruises and bloody wounds of my knees.

I was an altar boy at that time and used to carry the cross during funeral processions. The procession usually began in the house where the person died. Even today, the smell of Rosemary herbs placed around the casket to mask the stinking smell of the dead comes back to me. I always volunteered to carry the cross during the funeral processions because after the service we could go to the guest house to get food and eat.

I remember, at that time, I loved to attend a boys' club - until my father found out that it was a youth Nazi party and told me to stay away.

We were still living on that farm, slave refugees, when my appendix burst. I was ten years old. It took more than one hour for us to get to the hospital and my condition became deadly. The doctors told my mother that I wouldn't survive the surgery and suggested that she make arrangements for my funeral. After the surgery, I remained in the hospital for almost three months. I had a rubber tube coming out of my belly that was attached to a bag. This collected the liquid and fecal matter from my intestines. I had no solid food for two months, but I managed to survive.

I was eleven when I had to go and live with a farmer who had a guest house. I went from school to that house. My room was on top of a cow barn. The chief farm worker and I slept in the same place. Almost every night he would get the wooden ladder to visit some farmer's daughter (the farmers' daughters bedrooms were on the second floor). If the young lady objected to the visit, she would pour her chamber pot on his head.

My job at the farm was to take care of four big plowing horses. I had to rub them down with an iron brush; the horses were so docile they wouldn't harm a fly. I also cleaned their stalls and fed them.

I was about to go home on a Saturday night to be with my siblings. My brother, who was born on February 27, 1941, was working for another farmer. he also went home on Saturdays. My oldest brother was working further away, and he could only join us when he had the extra time.

I was coming down from the mountain one Saturday night pushing my bike. The ruts from the wagon's wheels prevented me from riding properly. It was getting dark. All of a sudden I looked straight ahead and saw a light moving near. Was it coming from a kerosene lantern? It wasn't. I watched it as it moved about, dancing up and down several times, until it finally disappeared. It was fascinating - and horrifying, too. I never did find out what it was. It wasn't the only strange thing that happened to me at that time.

My father used to be a road construction worker. He came home when they didn't have any work because of the Winter. Unfortunately, he became an alcoholic; he was drunk all the time he was home. He was verbally abusive to my mother. He threatened to kill her.

When my brother Joe and I came home on a Saturday night, my mother told us to get a rope to tie my father so he wouldn't fall off the sled. So, Joe and I went up to the guest house where he was drinking, and when we arrived, he had already passed out. We laid him down with his head in front of the sleigh, tied him down and put the sled - the sled with my father - on to a frozen path.

We had to go downhill for about a quarter of a mile. So, we gave the sled a push, and it picked up some speed. The sled went down so fast that we couldn't chase it fast enough to grab hold. It went right into the wall of our house, and our father's head crashed right into the wall. Bruises and a big bump were the price of his ride. Our mother knew what we had done, but she never said a word to our father until we came to America. Yes, perhaps, we deliberately did that to our father to change his mood or way of life. Perhaps we wanted to retaliate for all the times he threatened our mother. She passively withstood his debasing abusive words and never uttered a thing. Mother and father felt deep love for each other, and she had great compassion for all the trauma he had suffered in the wars. He had been sent there against his will; he was a young farmer who only wanted to be with his beloved wife and children.

I lived with the farmer almost up to the time when we came to America in April, 1956. I was nearly fourteen years old. We were supposed to have left for the *Land of Hope* in March, but at that time Soviet Russia invaded Hungary and many Hungarian refugees fearing for their lives preceded us to the United States. We had to wait an entire month at the Bremen Harbor in Germany.

My mother was an exceptionally gifted girl. Her parents were exceptionally skilled and kind-hearted farmers. She rode out all of the life-threatening events she went through. Her parents trained her to survive; she was a heroine who kept her family alive no matter what evil forces came our way.

She came up with all kinds of culinary ideas, creating meals, for her children from whatever she found, using pasture grass, mushrooms, and all sorts of berries. She would ask the farmers after they finished harvesting if she could pick up some missing grains, or corn from oak trees. A genuine survivor's spirit guided her to provide for all of us despite the poverty, scarcity, and an absent husband. She was there for all of us. With her bounteous and visionary attitude, three years before we came to America she had saved enough money to buy a house lot from an Austrian who had no problems with Yugoslav refugees. Other Austrians hated him because he was kind and supported the refugees.

With all of us putting our money together we were able, with the help of relatives and friends, to build a house.

It took my parents three years to gather all the documents we needed to come to the United States. The sale of the house paid for the trip to America. We had only three boxes, three feet by three feet each. We had everything we needed at that time: *"The dream to accomplish a better life as nothing else could have been worse than those years of slavery in our own land."* Our passage took eleven days, nine days of which I was very sick.

We arrived in New York City at night. It looked to us like a vast gigantic Christmas tree. I had never seen so many lights before. They put smiles on our faces. Here hope was alive and with that, the possibility of living the life we wanted to live at last. The next day we arrived at Ellis Island. There, we were sprayed like animals with some white powder which we guessed might have been for lice or other conditions. I remember that I was thirteen years and seven months old when we came to the United States. Then, for the first time, a new chapter of our life began. We were no longer slaves, refugees working for pennies and starving on the farms of others.

4

Becoming Americans

*"I am neither of the East nor of the West,
no boundaries exist within my breast."*

Rumi

My father's uncle who lived in the United States sponsored our immigration to America. The first three weeks we stayed at his house not far from Pearson's Corner, Delaware.

The agreement that my father had with his uncle was that we could stay at his farm and work for him for one year. The house on the farm was a very old house, but we had learned how to bring beauty to our lives.

My brother Joseph and I slept in one of the rooms upstairs. There was an old maple tree; black snakes would slither out of holes in that tree and come to invade our bedroom. We were scared of them at first, but after a while, we felt that they were not a threat and we even got used to them.

The farm was located on Rogers Corner Road and Melville Road, Delaware. The girls on the school bus wanted to sit with me but there wasn't enough room on the same seat. The school bus driver noticed all this and he would tell the girls to leave me alone. This was probably when I started thinking about the opposite sex. The fussing of the girls didn't bother me at all.

At first, as a newly arrived immigrant, the only word that I spoke in English was *"okay"*. I learned it from an American soldier while we were living in Austria. I knew that the soldier was from a country called America. By way of introduction he would point towards his chest: "American, American" he repeated and pointing to my chest he added: "German, German." We all laughed. Sensing my curiosity, my father shared with me what he had heard about the Americans. He told me, "They are free people!" I then asked my father: "Free from what, dad?" "Free to express themselves, free to have their own religion, to live in the culture that everyone wants to live, free to marry those who they want to marry...so free that sometimes they feel they must bring the freedom to other countries, to help innocent people escape the suffering of their wars."

I also asked him, "But why, if they want to help the suffering countries, did they drop bombs while we were expelled from Yugoslavia? We barely survived those attacks when we were fleeing from persecution."

My father replied, "We all make mistakes, son; sometimes wars create confusion and even those who come to help can end up hurting too. But we know that it was not their intention . . . the story is very long . . ."

While saying that, he stroked my blond hair and pulled me in to the warmth of his chest. I felt the strength of his arms and his love. I will always be grateful for his unconditional love, even though he had not biologically sired me.

We worked on his uncle's farm. We planted cauliflower

seedlings by hand for about 20 acres and when it was harvest time we put them into wooden crates. Mr. Petri would then take them to Philadelphia. As it has been a very wet year, the cauliflower had some black spots on them, so Mr. Petri couldn't get the best possible price. When we were done with the cauliflower, we went to work for a Polish farmer picking up tomatoes and putting them into half bushel baskets, stacking them like pyramids on the wagon.

One day, when I was picking tomatoes, I had a rotten tomato in my hand. I was about to throw it in the trash when I noticed a beautiful girl looking at me. When I returned her 7glanced she pretended she did not now noticed me. I had to get her attention, I threw the rotten tomato with uncanny precision: it landed right in her face. I thought I was done for: "perhaps — but no." Not only did she fail to complain, but she calmly waited until I was distracted then threw me a rotten tomato . . . that exploded on the side of my head. We looked at each other. Our two faces were now dripping tomato red. We didn't know it at the time, but that tomato battle was the beginning of a very long and accomplished life together.

Her family was also of German ethnicity. They were refugees from Hungary at the very same time we fled from Yugoslavia in November, 1944. They lived as refugees in Germany and came to America in 1952, four years before we did. The farm where they stayed was near Queen Avenue in Maryland.

We were milking about 40 cows a day. We had two milkers; we could milk two cows at the same time with these, and my mother, my brother Joe and I also milked by hand. By that time my oldest brother Johan was working in New Jersey.

My brother Joe was my best friend; we did everything together. We used to wrestle a lot. Sometimes we would have to get a cow

31

from the pasture, and we would get into an old pickup, driving with such speed that we mastered jumping the ditch. Sometimes we mastered jumping the ditch; other times we just fell in. We kept this adventure to ourselves; otherwise, our parents would not allow us to drive the pickup anymore.

Our parents had an extensive garden. We had to get up at 3:30 a.m. to get everything done before the school bus arrived. We were milking and feeding the animals, including the heifers, chickens and pigs. The full milk cans had to be loaded on a wagon; it took me and my brother Joe just to pick up a single milk can. When we were ready to go to school, we would drive the tractor pulling a wagon loaded with full milk cans to the end of our long driveway and put the milk cans onto a platform, then get on the school bus. On our way home, after school, the school bus would stop at the end of the lane. Joe and I put the empty milk cans back into the wagon and then went home.

My sisters Resi and Lisi went to a different school. After we got home from school, we had a sandwich: that would have to do until supper. Afternoon was the time for chores: milking, feeding, cleaning, and doing everything else we needed to do to finish all the chores before it got dark. After the hard farm work, we had to clean ourselves, had dinner and do our homework. During the week, we went to bed at nine and got up at 3:30 a.m. to start our day. Just thinking about those days, about all those chores, still gets me exhausted today. Not to mention when it was time for planting crops, cultivating, preparing the rolls of hay, and harvesting - how many more hours we needed to add to our days!

In 1958 there was a severe drought. It hardly rained and we had to buy hay from other farmers. My parents and the owner of the farm lost money because of the dry season. Next to the farm lived a Hungarian older couple who had a farm. They wanted my parents to buy it. Our parents asked Joe and I if we would like to stay with them if they bought that farm, but my brother and I replied at the same time: "No thank you!"

The dry year made our parents decide to move to Passaic, New Jersey, to a street called Hope Avenue. All along that street lived people from all over the world. Our landlord's family was Jewish, and they were always very kind to us. But not everyone was kind. There were a bunch of boys at school that made all sorts of *Nazi* remarks just because I spoke German. Sometimes a group of the Europeans' boys went to a park to play soccer; when I didn't show up someone from the school went to my house and accused me of truancy. My father got so angry that he hit me with his fist right on the side of my head. That was the last time he did that: as soon as I turned 16, I quit school for good.

My first job after moving to New Jersey was working for Julian's greenhouse. Hundreds of people worked there. I worked in the carpentry shop and did maintenance. I carried old wood on my shoulder that had been laying on the ground.

One sweltering hot day, I wasn't wearing a shirt. A black widow spider crawled on my shoulder and stung me a poison sting. They had to take me to the hospital where I stayed overnight. I worked at the greenhouse for about a year and a half. Later, I found another job that paid much more than the greenhouse. The company that hired me made all sorts of lamps. My job was to assemble them.

I found a section in the plant where people painted the bottom of porcelain ceramics using oil paint. I watched them with great interest. One day during my lunch break, one of the painters said, "You look like someone who is very interested in doing this." I replied that I used to paint with watercolors. "This is much easier than it is with watercolors," he said. I told him that a friend of mine in Austria and I used to compete painting Christmas cards, Easter cards, and landscape paintings. Then, during one lunch break, I was invited to paint the bottom of a lamp. It was great! Blending the oil colors inspired me, and I found myself really enjoying this work. My interest in painting and art started when I was about nine years old. I still devote time to painting my inspirations in oil, even to today.

My next job was at Winkler Textile. My brother Joe and I used to compound paint for the printers by using paint that came in powder and adding a creamy substance. When the sun shone through the window panes, the powder in the air made visible rainbows. We were not aware that we were breathing it in. My coughing became so severe that the doctor warned me that if I continued working there, I might soon be dead. Back then, people were not especially concerned about the health of their workers.

When I turned 18, I met a person in a bar. Over his beer, he told me that he and his father were looking for someone who could assist a chemist. He was vice president for a company that did work for the federal government. He recommended me to his father who interviewed me. I got the job.

It was just the chemist and me working in a laboratory. The chemist would give me formulas that I had to follow. Our job was to find out how to chemically plate copper on a material made of natural mica and gypsum.

I performed thousands of trials combining a variety of chemicals, varying the length of time in the solution, varying the temperature, the water, and other factors. I learned that our work was private, highly secure - but the chemist in charge went to jail for selling secret information.

Another chemist was a British man who was arrested for speeding. He drove in excess of 100 mph and would not stop; when the police finally caught him, the judge gave him three months in jail. To make things worse a lunatic took his place: we were already behind schedule. The high security works were for the first orbital flight.

On several occasions, the entire plant had to be evacuated. When some formula exploded, they would rush into the lab, grab me and take me to a hosedown area where they stripped off my clothes and scrubbed me down. I had to wear special hazard clothes to prevent any harm to me when these situations arose. While working there, I took night classes to learn chemistry and electro-mechanical crafting.

I didn't particularly care that I was followed wherever I went. I was only 19. I began dating the same young lady of the rotten tomato episode. I married Elisabeth, on May 5, 1962. We lived in Clifton, New Jersey.

In October, 1962 I received a letter from the draft board. I would be drafted in March of 1963. I went to the recruiting office in Paterson, New Jersey to find out if I could enlist in the Army instead of being drafted. The Army recruiter said that if I joined by November 18th, 1962, he could guarantee me Europe.

I immediately accepted that offer and went to Fort Dix, New Jersey for basic training. On one occasion, we had to go through a chlorine gas chamber. We entered the gas chamber in full gear, wearing all the necessary combat paraphernalia to be prepared for combat. The gas mask hung in a pouch on the side of my leg. I had to enter the gas chamber *not wearing a gas mask,* but holding my breath, while the instructor inside asked me for the serial number of my weapon. I didn't have the correct serial number on my weapon, and the instructor wouldn't allow me to put on my gas mask. The next thing I remember was being outside, laying on the ground while they gave me oxygen. This took place a few days before graduation from basic training. I ended up hospitalized, severely ill from the chlorine gas I inhaled. After arriving at Fort Lee, Virginia Army base, I spent my first two weeks in the hospital. According to the doctor exposure to the chlorine gas had changed my blood. Chlorine gas chambers were eventually discontinued because so many soldiers were ill or even died from exposure.

After finishing at quartermaster's school at Fort Lee, I received orders to report on April 10, 1963 to Idlewild Airport, from where I would fly to Milan, Italy for duty in Vicenza, Italy. My first assignment at cold storage was to record the temperature twice a day outside the icebox units. That's how I came to be known as "the icebox man". I was now Private First Class Fueller.

The sergeant in charge was a world war soldier, an alcoholic about to retire. He was the second person to be in charge of the cold storage unit, but drank more than the one he had replaced. We both became best friends as did our wives.

Gregory P. had been a first sergeant during World War II. Because of his drinking problem, he was demoted to the rank of staff sergeant. Soon after, he was put in charge of cold storage. A lieutenant from a missile unit came with his men to pick up rations for their mess hall. The lieutenant said that he was in a hurry; Sergeant Gregory P. remarked that there were others in front of him and that he would have to wait.

Nonetheless, the lieutenant demanded to be taken care of immediately. At that moment, Gregory P. lost his patience. Gregory P. took the lieutenant by his neck and by his belt and threw him out of the office. The lieutenant landed on his face on the concrete floor. When the military was done with Gregory

P., they had reduced him to the rank of Private First Class; he would be allowed to finish his military time in retirement, which was within the year. Gregory P.'s job during World War II was in grave registration; he said that he could see the dead soldiers as ghost spirits, flying all around him. He put each dead soldier's dog tag in between their teeth.

My company commander promoted me to temporary acting Corporal. I was in charge of five Italian civilians and nine soldiers. He would pick up a uniform from the laundromat then come to the section of cold storage where the perishable products (including four bottles of whiskey) were kept. My commander knew where these bottles were, took several gulps, then returned the following Wednesday. He also had been a World War II soldier, and during the war, his platoon leader was killed. He received a battlefield commission to be second lieutenant by the Congress of the United States. My company commander was one of the best commanders I have served under. My wife Elisabeth didn't come to Italy right away. She arrived in Milan by the end of May, and I was supposed to meet her at the Milan airport, but my train arrived at the train station very late. I couldn't find her. I was told that the bus from the airport had already left; even when the bus arrived, my wife wasn't on the bus. The U.S.O. called me and said that she had arrived and had been retained at the Italian Immigration office. They held her because she entered the country without a passport, but she had a copy of my orders that I had given to her before I left to come to Italy. She was six months pregnant and was crying non-stop. After talking to the immigration officers, I convinced them that she was my wife and before releasing her they demanded that she get her passport within the month.

I was required to be a Sergeant in order for us to live in

military housing, but I was only a Corporal. I told my company commander that my wife had arrived in Italy. He was concerned that we had to live off base, but I assured him that we would be fine: we were originally from Europe. There were times when I had to translate for the company commander when German young men who didn't speak English were drafted.

My wife and I found an apartment right in the city of Vicenza, and we enjoyed living there surrounded by our Italian neighbors. We had our ice cream man, the wine man, and the bread man. They invited us to spend time with their large families and relish the tasty Italian food, the wine and, of course, their great seasonal salamis.

I bought a 1954 Ford car from a soldier who had returned to America. The car needed to be repaired and painted. It came just at the right time: my wife had our baby boy on August 29, 1963. We named him Ferdinand, III. He was born weighing in at ten pounds. He was the biggest baby ever born in the Army Hospital.

Our company commander and his wife were wonderful people. They organized parties, birthday's parties, as well as, Easter and Christmas celebrations for the soldiers' families.

On Friday, November 22, 1963, President Kennedy was assassinated. All the soldiers that were living off base and in military housing had to report to their units on post. We were not allowed to go home to our families. All of the units were on standby, ready for combat. While we were on standby, the military unit that was responsible for our families brought them to Aviano Air Force Base and put them on airplanes to return to the United States; they were also on standby. We were unaware that they moved them to Aviano Air Force Base. Several days later, the alert was lifted and everything went back to the way it was before.

Our best friend Robert and his wife from Morgantown, West

Virginia were born in the United States. Although they lived in Italy, they didn't speak Italian. They lived on the base not too far from where we lived, and we did a lot of things together with camaraderie and great family spirit.

When Robert screwed up, Captain Capelli called him into his office. Robert went scratching his head, thinking of how to convince the Captain that it hadn't been his fault.

Our unit also supported other units when missile units were practicing war games not far from the Austrian mountains. Robert would drive a gas tanker. He also used to drive a perishables truck. The missile unit that was supposed to receive these supplies was about four hours away. Robert said that he had to use the bathroom and we stopped at the nearest town, but after that, he went to the bar and had a beer. One beer wasn't enough for either of us; we spent the night at the bar. When Captain Capelli called, wanting to know why we haven't delivered the supplies to the missile units, Robert told the captain that the perishables truck had broken down and we needed to replace a tire. All these issues put us behind schedule.

When we arrived at the missile unit, the Major from that unit said that he would court-martial me because I was the one in charge of that mission. Captain Capelli wouldn't approve the Major's order to have me court-martialed. Six months later the same Major came to our unit to party, demanding that someone get his food. I approached the Major and told him to go to the end of the line. Again he threatened me with a court-martial. Captain Capelli, heard what the Major said, came over and told him to get the hell out of my unit.

The quartermaster is responsible for everything from food, finances, ammunition, toilet paper, and everything else necessary for the operation and our life there.

My wife, now two months pregnant, together with our six months old son Ferdinand III, and I went to visit our relatives in Austria and Germany.

When we arrived at the Austrian border, the border patrol requested me to open the trunk and saw the five cans of gas. They wouldn't allow us to bring them in. We had to cross Austria through the mountains and it was snowing very hard. To make things worse, the road was slippery. My car didn't have any traction, so I couldn't continue driving. We left the car halfway down the mountain, carried our son, and walked up the mountain where there was a guest house. I explained to the people there what had just happened, and four men volunteered to go down to where my car was, and we brought the vehicle to the guest house. They wouldn't take any money for their help, but I was able to toast them with a round of beer for all. They were wonderful people.

In the morning, we decided to continue our trip. The first relative we visited was my mother's youngest brother's wife (Schtefan Pschenizer). Her husband had not volunteered to be an SS officer; he came back home from Russia - never willing to return.

My mother's older sister's husband, a member of the German secret police, pointed a gun at Schtefan's head and ordered him to return to his unit in Russia. When he went back, he told his soldiers to surrender to the Russian military, as he knew that it was only a matter of time before Germany would lose the war. When he surrendered with his men, the Russian soldiers shot him in his head right in front of his men. Then, his men went to Siberia and only two of them survived the war.

Six years later, when those two men were released as war prisoners, they were not allowed to go back to Yugoslavia;

instead, they had to go to Germany. That's when they found out what happened to Schtefan. My aunt had two children and her daughter was wounded. She had a piece of shrapnel in her brain inflicted from an American bomb dropped while we were fleeing to save our lives in a convoy with a horse-drawn wagon.

When we visited our family in Austria, my aunt told us she had cancer. She loved to hug our son, Ferdinand III. We had a wonderful time visiting them.

The next relatives we visited were one of my mother's sisters and her husband. They lived in Bruchsal, Germany. It was a bitter experience knowing that he was the one who sent his brother-in-law Schtefan to get killed by the Russians when he obliged him to return to Russia. When we were with this family, my aunt's husband left the room, and we didn't see him again. He couldn't stand the idea that I was an American soldier. On the contrary, my aunt and her children were very kind to us.

The last relatives that we visited on that trip were from my wife Elisabeth's side.

They were intimately familiar with all that we have suffered during our horrendous times as refugees. They were victims too. They were also of German ethnicity.

My father-in-law was a Hungarian citizen before World War II. He had to serve in the German army, but not by choice. He was captured by the Russians and sent to Siberia as a war prisoner. Later, he was not allowed to return to Hungary and was sent to Germany instead. During Tito's dictatorship, the ethnic Germans and Hungarians from former Yugoslavia were not allowed to return to what was once Yugoslavia. In 1946, Tito demanded that all the property of ethnic Germans was to be confiscated and given to his partisan fighters. The ethnic Germans lost their citizenship, too.

41

During those terrible times, Elisabeth's mother and sister had been repeatedly raped by the Russian army or by Tito's partisans. My wife's mother buried Elisabeth when she was two years old to prevent the Russian military from raping her. When her mother went back to get her daughter (my wife), she almost died from suffocation.

One of my Elisabeth's sisters married my oldest brother. He was 12 years old when we had to flee from Yugoslavia. He remembers seeing what Tito's partisans and their collaborators had done to ethnic Germans. When they caught an ethnic German boy or a man, they would cut them from the navel all the way up to the chest, exposing their internal organs and leaving them to die.

My wife has two more siblings, a brother who was born in Germany and another sister who was born in the United States.

5

But I Didn't Die in Vietnam

"The only journey is the one within."

Rainer Maria Rilke

After visiting our relatives in Austria and Germany, we returned to my military unit in Italy.

Letters were waiting for me from the Austrian government. One of the letters said that I had been drafted into the Austrian army as a second lieutenant and had only 30 days to report to military service (after living in Austria for 11 years as refugees, they made me an Austrian citizen). The U.S. Army's attorney responded to the Austrian government: I could not serve in Austria's military force because I still had six months of military obligation with the U.S. Army, and I would be sent back to the U.S. to finish my time there. When I returned to the United States, the Austrian government no longer had jurisdiction to draft me for military service.

On September 28, 1964, we had a girl, and we named her Santina (Tina), inspired by our neighbor friend in Italy. She was my birthday present; she was born the same calendar day as me.

Sometime in the middle of January, 1965, my company commander asked me to stay in Italy until my three years of active duty was completed, but Captain Capelli said he already had the orders for me to report to Fort Polk, Louisiana.

I was scheduled to leave on March 4, 1965, on a flight from Milan, Italy to New York. They gave me 30 days to leave. I was to report on April 5, 1965, to Fort Polk, Louisiana - and probably go to Vietnam. I reminded Captain Capelli that I only had six months left of the 3 years of military obligation and that Vietnam would be one more year. Moreover, I was entitled to decline serving in the Vietnam war, since I wasn't a citizen yet. They could not send me to combat unless I volunteered. I told him that I'd talk to my wife and let him know our decision. After I talked to our parents and my wife, we decided to return to the United States. The Italian friends and some other friends organized a memorable goodbye party.

A person in the military traveling from one assignment to another has to be dressed in uniform. When my family and I arrived in New York City, the people at the airport treated me with disrespect. Some of them spat on me and called me a baby killer. I didn't understand why. I never killed an innocent person; I never killed anyone! I was in the military duty doing what I was required to do. Once at home, I found out why there was so much hatred against soldiers.

When I was in Italy, they didn't want us to know about the animosity towards the United States military. But the facts about the United States' involvement in Vietnam, about the massacres and slaughter of innocents, were known worldwide.

At first, I was not impressed by the anti-war movement. It was a different story when I later learned what had really happened in Vietnam. The hippies and anti-war demonstrators were right in blaming America for making the bad situation in Vietnam even worse: terrible irreparable damage to human rights that brought disastrous consequences for both the Vietnamese and the poor young American soldiers who were forced to participate in the atrocities of that war.

I have known veterans that had been pilots in Vietnam and received orders to bomb the same spot year after year. They said that they knew that there were no North Vietnamese soldiers there.

Arriving at Fort Polk, Louisiana on April 24, 1965, there were hundreds of us in an auditorium being brainwashed, by the recruiters, giving us reasons why we should let them extend our time to a one-year length so they could send us to Vietnam. The program was all about God and the Country, and it never showed us anything about the soldiers being killed in Vietnam. I didn't see anybody standing up to accept the idea of extending the program, which meant going to the Vietnam war. I didn't stand up either. Then I had to meet a recruiter who asked me to permit him to extend my time for a one-year commitment in Vietnam. I told him that I wouldn't allow that, and I knew my rights to deny such a proposal. He responded that he could send me anyway and I said that he could not because I wasn't an American citizen and; therefore, I can't be sent in combat without my consent. He angrily asked me to leave his office.

On April 24, 1965, I was assigned to Company A, 98th Bn (GS) at Fort Polk, Louisiana to work at a butchering facility. I didn't have any training for this. My job was to dissect bone meat, slice bacon, grind meat, and unload trucks filled with pigs. Balancing the pork on my shoulder and carrying it into the cooler where it was ground into sausage, was hard work. I would not eat meat in the mess hall at all.

A little while later, after starting at the butcher place, I was walking back to the barracks and to my surprise found T. Miller in front of me, telling me that in a few days he would be going to Vietnam. He was a party man who never married and who had belonged to my unit in Italy; he was a pothead and most of the time he asked me for money until he got paid. Many friends from cold storage were sent to Vietnam. T. Miller got killed on a patrol one week after he arrived in Vietnam.

Because I refused to go to Vietnam, they ordered me to do jobs that were not my duty, like working on weekends and holidays, and doing guard duty. The army was harassing me. The platoon sergeant would come into my room at two or three in the morning and blow a whistle right into my ear. Enough harassment, I picked up my boot and threw it hitting the back of his head. He went down on the floor.

The platoon sergeant told the first sergeant what I had done, and said he was going to court-martial me. I went to the Internal Generals and told them what had happened. A lieutenant with an Internal General had been assigned to me. The attorney asked me how long after he blew the whistle I had thrown the boot at the platoon sergeant.

I said, "Immediately, perhaps two seconds!" The lieutenant said not to worry about it since they cannot do anything to a person who has just woken up because there is a period of thirty seconds of lack of full awareness. Because of the harassment, I went to see the chaplain. He suggested that I write a letter to my congressman explaining what was happening. I did write a letter to my congressman, but never heard back from him.

My chronological record of military service documented that

from June 1, 1965, to July 6, 1965 I served in the Army. I don't recall what I had done during that time. From July 7, 1965, to September 24, 1965, I was assigned to Cel 98th QM Bn (GS) and from September 25 to November 14, 1965, with CoC, Sp Trps (4010). I was in charge of the Army reserve and National Guards units while they were at Fort Polk, Louisiana.

There were two weeks of training. I picked up their supplies. There were so many that had also refused to go to Vietnam who were in the same position that I was while I was waiting to get out of the Army. They made sure that they had refrigerators to keep their beer cold and played cards until they got released.

Three days before I was supposed to be discharged from the Army, I went to headquarters to get my discharge papers and was told that my 201 File was with a Combat Engineer Unit that has been sent to Vietnam. I asked how that was possible, but the person had no any explanation. In order for me to be discharged from active Army duty, they gave me temporary discharge papers. While I was leaving, the first sergeant told me that I wouldn't get out when I was supposed to, and I replied, "Check the logbook!"

After being discharged, I had nightmares of being dropped from a helicopter on a war field on the side of a cable bridge. I remember that all the other soldiers that were on the plane had their battle and survival equipment, but I had none. I also did not have much awareness of what was happening to me, but I did have a vivid sense that I was in serious danger and did not have any weapons to defend myself or survival equipment. I didn't know where I was or how I got there. But, my recurrent nightmares seemed to want me to release the traumatic stress I had lived through and from which I 'miraculously' had survived. In my recurrent and very scary dream I recalled the same experience:

"After being pushed out of a helicopter, I landed on a field close to a cable bridge. Later, I was running over to the other side of the bridge, the side of the bridge where the cable was attached to the concrete. When I placed an explosive device a soldier approached me, his weapon pointed at me. He said something I didn't understand, and I felt he wasn't friendly. Suddenly he looked away long enough for me to grab his weapon. The weapon fell to the ground. We started a fight, each trying to choke the other. That's when the explosive device that I had planted exploded, knocking us down to the bottom of the river. The riverbed was filled with big boulders. Unfortunately, for my opponent he hit his head on one and died bathing the rock with his blood. I heard two explosions coming from the other side of the bridge. I looked and saw a bunch of soldiers shooting at the helicopter. There was an exchange of fire between the soldiers and the helicopter. I looked up. I heard soldiers yelling at me with anger - I was next to the dead soldier on the boulder. The helicopter was leaving me behind. I had no way to escape, so I used the lifeless body of the soldier as a floating raft and made my way down the river until I was sure that no one was around. I went to the shore with his body. Once there, I searched him and found a photo of a young woman with a boy. Probably his family, I thought. I pulled him up to a place where he could be found."

In the dream, I had no idea how long or how far I walked. I don't even remember how I was found and when I got back to Fort Polk, nor did I recall having been in Vietnam. And yet, I would have the same nightmare about the bridge for many, many years.

My wife and I were sponsors for military veterans. Most of

these veterans were from World War II and the Korean War.

While I was with active Army reserve, my MOS was for supply sergeant and chemical biological weapons. My last assignment was at Fort Carson, Colorado, where I was exposed to all sorts of gases, viruses, and bacteria, all potential causes of serious medical disorders. I needed my medical records from St. Louis, Missouri (where all military records are kept), but they said that I was reported as Missing in Action (MIA) when I was with the Combat Engineer Unit that was sent to Vietnam. I had to prove to them that I was alive so that I could receive medical help from the VA. I shouted loudly, "No, I didn't die in Vietnam! I don't even remember that I ever agreed to go there!"

I remained in the Army active reserve for another 11 years completing 14 years of total military service.

After returning home from active military duty, I joined the Army Reserve 315th S&S C (Ds) in Dover, Delaware. My duty was to be active at the end of each month for two days, and two weeks with an active Army post in a different location throughout the United States every year. Two days a month with the Army Reserve provided me with a new source of income.

My supply company and I would go to Aberdeen Proving Ground and fill requisitions for units located there. I also took some of the reservists to the Edgewood chemical facility to fill orders - but only if they had experience in Chemistry. We lived with Elisabeth's parents until we found our first home. It was an old house that needed repair. While I was working on the first house we bought, I was also working for a housing builder as a carpenter. I had a lot of experience building greenhouses.

In 1977 I was still in the active reserve, and they sent me to Fort Carson, Colorado for training in chemical and biological warfare. I was exposed to all sorts of chemicals. I was a supply sergeant at the time but had not volunteered for that assignment. Before we left Maryland, I was about to be promoted to Master Sergeant, but the civilian administrator talked to the company commander into giving the Master Sergeant position to his friend. His request was accepted. They told me that when I came back from Fort Carson and took the position as a chemical and biological NCO, I would receive my promotion to Master Sergeant.

While I was being trained at Fort Carson, I had to handle a variety of different biological gases. I'd been in training for over a week and we were at the NCO Club with the instructors. There, one of the instructors noticed that I had twitches in my neck and arms. He asked me how long I had them and I said that I noticed them before. He examined my safety suit, and found a crack underneath the armpit. There was always a harmful agent in those test rooms. The suits were designed to prevent anything from penetrating the fabric. We also wore a headgear mask. If it hadn't been for the mask, I might have died. Exposure to biological gases caused nerve damage in my neck, arms, and chest.

When it was humid and cold, it felt like my nerves were short-circuiting. It was particularly excruciating during the period immediately following the accidental exposure. I would fill up the bathtub with hot water and hastily climb in to relieve the pain. The pain was especially severe in my chest, and I went to bed before the pain started again.

By the end of 1977, my agreement with the active reserve was over, and I left without receiving the promotion they promised me I would have. My rank when I left was Staff Sergeant (E6). I received three honorable discharges: one for three years of regular Army service and two for the Army active reserve. I devoted a total of 14 years in the military.

6

How Did I Become an Ex-Enemy at 4 and a half Years Old?

"Collective fear stimulates herd instinct and tends to produce ferocity toward those who are not regarded as members of the herd."

Bertrand Russell

Below is the abhorrent 'qualification' that describes me: first of all as an 'enemy' and then later, an 'ex-enemy'. How can a four and a half year old boy ever be an 'ex-enemy'?

EX-ENEMY 258630
DP IDENTIFICATION CARD
FULLER FERDINAND
Date-of-birth 29/9/42 - Age 4 1/2 - HEIGHT 94"
Weight 14 - Hair Blond - Eyes Blue
Nationality Yugoslav - DP Registration No. 203.449

All kind of discriminatory labels, labels that produce deep wounds in the psyche, become very difficult to eradicate in the culture. Discrimination plays its macabre role in the harassment of other human beings. Discrimination can justify and provoke extermination: psychological extermination and/or the physical extermination of another human being through an act of disintegration.

Victims of discrimination end up as disintegrated shards of society. It is as if that human being, had no right to belong to this planet. Discrimination not only destroys a target generation, but its malignant effects reappear in the following generations as a poisoned cascade of separatism, alienation and social marginalization. Unfortunately, disintegrating those considered unworthy of being members of society begins as a doctrine inculcated in the minds of children and reinforced within the family and in schools. Societies may label a person by judging his or her ethnicity or the line from which they descend in order to 'stereotype' them as worthy or unworthy of being integrated into the culture that is considered the 'majority', while the worthless remain living stagnant in the culture classified as the 'minority'.

Bigotry judges others as if they were lepers. It constantly promotes all kinds of racist feelings in children and adults against each other. The bricks of hatred build impenetrable walls and justify leaving behind, delivered to their miserable destiny, those considered from childhood as 'marginalized.'

Accumulated hatred towards others marks them as cattle. When seen as animals, killing them does not create a feeling of guilt or repentance. It may even seem justified. Do most people suffer when they kill a little piglet, a small calf, or a little lamb? No. Do most people suffer when they kill a baby snake or a cockroach that is growing? No. This is the mindset that expiates the guilt of those who, without hesitation or remorse, kill children and innocents because they are born 'of a certain abominable ethnicity.' Very few feel pain or shame for butchering little animals because they 'belong to the animal kingdom.' In the same way, a child that has been labeled as 'enemy' or 'ex-enemy' bears the stigma of being devalued, discriminated and perhaps massacred without any remorse on the part of their executioners. Since the beginning of recorded history children have been horribly tormented and killed because they were Jews, or because they were Muslims, or because they were Germans, or belonged to a different African or Asian tribe. They had to be eliminated because they were unacceptable, ethnically abominable, and did not deserve to live.

Back to my story . . . During my very early years, I wondered why the United States was bombing us when we, the innocent population living in former Yugoslavia, and had to flee to Austria to escape from extermination. We fled. We fled in fear, in disconsolate anguish, with the deep pain of leaving the life we used to know, to love, and grew up in.

The burden was even greater, since we did not know what we might expect in the very uncertain future. We were refugees hoping to survive the constant bombing that threatened our lives as we fled along with others in the long caravans on horseback.

I never thought that the United States considered us an enemy after World War II. Just because a dictatorship or government (in this case, the Third Reich) created a war, slaughtering innocent people to achieve its ultimate purpose, does not mean that all ethnic Germans have been or were Nazis. However, many Germans in some parts of the world have been labeled as Nazis by narrow-minded people treating them in very aggressive and vengeful ways. That is why many innocents, who have not taken part in a war's actions made by their governments, nonetheless suffered terrifying reprisals against children, women, or any and

53

every one considered not part of that ethnic group.

Great Britain and the former Soviet Union accused and made responsible 'all' the ethnic Germans for what the Nazi party in Germany had done to the Jews and other victims, including those compassionate people who were not Jews but who helped them to flee or hide.

The United States, Great Britain, and the former Soviet Union supported the bloodbath terrorist movement against a recognized country - Yugoslavia. They already knew that the executioner Tito was exterminating ethnic Germans in a massive genocidal sweep; this knowledge had been secretly hidden from the rest of the world. Not many people were aware of what had happened to those considered of German origin. The three major powers at that time remained silent, absent, and distant while Tito continued to slaughter innocent civilians of every age who were ethnic Germans - long after the second World War ended.

There is hardly any factual material available in the United States, Great Britain, or in Russia, documenting what happened to the ethnic Germans and to all six countries that have once been Yugoslavia.

Tito passed a law in 1945 that all the properties of the ethnic Germans were to be given to the partisan fighters, supporters, and followers of his regimen. Over 70 years later that law is as 'valid' as it was then.

Josip Broz, alias 'Tito', took over Yugoslavia in 1945 and he ruled as a dictatorship until his death in 1980. He manipulated the Leninist doctrine to gain power and the trust of people in former Yugoslavia. He took advantage of the information he managed to receive from the Communist secret police to become the commander of Belgrade, right after World War II. Following this he subjected the young Balkan nation to his absolute authoritarian control, making it a one-party system run by him. It was the beginning of his bloody and very astute dictatorship.

As soon as he learned that Moscow was about to take control of his growing power, Tito cut his ties with Stalin and started lobbying with the countries of the West, dropping hints about "the non-communist type of government he was about to develop." But as soon as the countries of the West obliged him to create fair elections based on a multi-party system, Tito betrayed the western countries and started his long years of criminal dictatorial power.

Besides the concentration camps where he massacred civilians refugees of all ages, he created what he called "penitentiaries" to warehouse those who opposed his regime. Many political opponents and dissidents couldn't leave the country and were obliged to work as slaves. Among one of his worse "penitentiaries" was the one in Goli Otok - the Naked Island - that mimicked the same barbarous and inhumane rites as Stalin's death camps.

Tito ruled as an absolute dictator for 37 years; during that time, hundreds of thousands were rounded up and severely punished for speaking against his regime or for daring to voice their opposition. One of his victims was a pacifist student movement leader, Ivan Zvonimir Cicak. In 1971, Cicak had advocated the democratization of Yugoslavia. Tito harshly punished him and others like him. Mr. Cicak later became the head of the Croatian Helsinki Committee for Human Rights and received an award from the country's president in 2015. In his own words, "Tito was a criminal and a dictator, similar to Franco. He survived both Hitler and Stalin and slightly modified their Fascism and Communism." A Kosovo Albanian writer called Adem Demaci, had been sentenced to 28 years as a political prisoner until he was released by the Croatian authorities as Yugoslavia started to crumble. He later won the Sakharov Prize, an award from the European Parliament that honors individuals who devote their lives to support the defense of freedom and human rights.

At that time and perhaps still today, Tito made people believe that he was the architect of the Socialist regime with a humanitarian "care" for his country.

The famous Israeli writer Ephraim Kishon, who had been in the Holocaust and is a Communism survivor, said that Marshal Tito tricked his citizens into believing that "they had a better life with a little bit of freedom". This of course was pure hype, a smoke screen allowing him to continue his horrendous bloodshed against those who opposed him.

Tito was smart and bloody enough to maintain internal cohesion, suppressing every nationalistic movement during the constitution of the six republics: Bosnia and Herzegovina, Croatia, Macedonia, Montenegro, Slovenia, Serbia, and two autonomous provinces, Kosovo and Vojvodina.

At the beginning of Tito's dictatorship, the ethnic Germans had to flee. As a result, their homes, businesses, farms, and other properties were expropriated by Tito's partisans.

The majority of ethnic Germans haven't been able to file for restitution of property. This is because Tito's partisans stole their titles, birth certificates, and other important documents in order to prevent the possibility of restitution claims. In my case, whether Divine Providence, or my mother, intervened in 1941. She had been perceptive and wise enough to save the titles and documents that prove we own the properties that had been expropriated from us. She had a talent for hiding documents. She tucked away all the documents that established our identities, as well as, the titles of all the properties that we legitimately possessed from our work and through the inheritance from our grandparents. She hid them inside the large feather cushion on which I was lying when I was two years old as we fled from our agonizing Yugoslavia towards Austria.

The partisans stopped us on the road and checked everything, looking for our documents, but they found nothing. My mother said they did not want to move me from the cushion because I was crying a lot. No doubt: Divine Providence was already protecting us. We not only escaped the bombs dropped by the planes on the caravans of civilians, but we also kept those documents that today allow us, perhaps after a long process, to recover what was once ours in our former Yugoslavia. Only those ethnic Germans who have been able to save their property documents can claim their rights; but, even so, the people who stole their properties still manage to create terrible delays and ironclad bureaucracies to prevent the legitimate owners from reclaiming their property.

If my parents would have told me that the United States was bombing us while we were fleeing from the partisans, I am not certain whether I would have been willing to serve in the United States Army. They were trying to kill me when I was two years old! Maybe I would have done what so many others did: they went to Canada before receiving the call to be drafted into the Army and thrown into the war.

I have served the United States of America's Army to the best of my ability and with love for this country. For me it was an honor to help defend the USA against any of its enemies.

In order to be allowed to come to the United States in 1956, one had to sign an agreement obliging service in the United States military. So for me, serving in the United States military became a 'must do' - or flee. Fight or flight, the very same trigger of our internal stress response system.

I know that ever since I was conceived, some Higher Power has been watching over me; somehow my life has been protected from any premature death. So, after all is said and done, I believe that I would have agreed to serve in the United States military. After all, they accepted us as refugees when our Yugoslavian uncle, already an American citizen, asked us to come to live on his farm. Members of my family are still today bearing the wounds resulting from those bombs dropped on us as we fled. My cousin Theresa Resi, who lives in Austria, stile has a piece of shrapnel in her brain. My cousin Stephen in Nebraska has undergone five surgery to treat wounds he received from an American bomb.

Nevertheless, I still stand opposed to the authoritarian military bureaucracy that forced me to go to Vietnam when I had every right not to. I was not an American citizen then; therefore, I could have only be sent as a volunteer, it was only a matter of months before my years of commitment to the United States Army would end. I already served the necessary time in the Army, with only six months of military duty remaining. That's why I didn't give them permission to extend my service to a one-year stint in Vietnam. However, after I didn't accept going to Vietnam, they forced me to go 'their way': they drugged me to the point of insensibility. I became a mindless passive zombie acting without will and without consciousness of what was happening. They put me on a plane, and then in a helicopter, and sent me without weapons or any survival backpack to a battlefield in Vietnam.

God wanted me to come back alive and that in itself was a divine miracle. But from the depths of my unconsciousness, through recurrent nightmares, I eventually became aware of where I had been and what I had done while drugged. The pictures in my dreams became more clear and more real, nightmare after nightmare.

I remember in my recurrent nightmares that I was walking onto the airplane without my combat readiness gear on. Unlike everyone else, I had no duffel bag. The nightmares revealed everything I had lived through; meanwhile, the Army told me that I had been declared dead in combat in Vietnam.

When I needed to present my official documents to the Veteran Administration, I contacted an officer in charge in St. Louis, Missouri (where they kept all the military documents). The person at the office told me that I had died in action. I had much to do to prove to them that I had not died, and that I needed to be officially recognized as a veteran who had honorably served the United States of America.

I remember now in detail what happened after the helicopter dropped me off. It has been many years since that incident, but there is no doubt in my mind now that it did happen.

I need to express my own opinion regarding my classification as an ex-enemy at the age of 4 1/2. First of all, my ancestry as an ethnic German had nothing to do with the country known as Germany. The country that I was born in was Yugoslavia, and Croatia was part of Yugoslavia. My birth certificate verifies that I was born in Yugoslavia.

Between 1945 and 1948, first the Russians, then, the United States and Great Britain, supported Tito's atrocious barbarities against the ethnic Germans. The ethnic Germans had been taken as hostages and slaves to survive in the unthinkable hell of the concentration and extermination camps. I was there. I lived the horrifying story firsthand. I am not writing it here because I am repeating events that have been told to me. Moreover, I am the illegitimate son of a young woman who was repeatedly raped by

Tito's partisans. I am living proof of the horrendous torment that we, the Germanic ethnic group born in former Yugoslavia, have suffered. I was issued a card stating that I was an 'ex-enemy' when I was only 4 1/2 years old; this was the same time they supported Tito's bloody actions against people of all ages, children, women, pregnant, the young and elderly - anyone who belonged to the German ethnic race.

The world has to know what the three major powers did to the ethnic Germans, so it doesn't happen again!

7

Joe, my Beloved Brother and my Best Friend

"When brothers agree, no fortress is so strong as their common life."

Antisthenes

When we arrived in Austria as refugees, we were under the Russian military, then the French military, and later under the American military. Whenever the Americans stationed in our area, my brother Joe and I would go after what they had left and dug up the holes that they covered up hoping that we could find food. Sometimes we managed to find edible food. I pray to God that my children, grandchildren, great-grandchildren, and any children in the world never have to suffer as we did. My stomach hurt most of the time because I was always hungry.

Both my brother Joe and I were inseparable. We always watched out for one another because of the hatred we regularly received from the Austrian boys since we were refugees.

When we came to America, Joe and I would always work together, whether it was our uncle's farm, as migrant workers, at a dairy farm, at the greenhouse, or at Winkler Textile mixing paint. We attended night classes together at a local college. Joe had a brilliant mind, much smarter than mine. He pursued electronic engineering, and I took mechanical/electrical drafting and chemistry.

At the local college, Joe met a professor who told him that he needed to smoke marijuana to be more extroverted and express himself freely. Joe bought the idea of becoming more extroverted and started smoking pot. When Joe smoked marijuana inside our apartment, I would get terrible headaches but I supported Joe's choices and never judged him. I just didn't like to smoke it. We were both naive and never expected that smoking marijuana could lead to a severe habit or could act as a gateway to other drugs. Today, the consumption of marijuana, for recreational and medicinal use, has become legal in over thirty states, but it wasn't legal when my brother was persuaded by his teacher to start smoking the weed. Unfortunately for Joe, he not only did he succumb to the habit of smoking marijuana, but he also developed addictions to other more dangerous drugs. The bright flame of his mind began to slowly fade the deeper he fell into the depressive states caused by drugs. He became a boy who, without losing his big heart or his warm attitude began to collapse psychologically. He made frequent suicidal attempts.

Joe was in charge of the farm and took care of our parents as well. My parents were concerned and distressed, fearing that the worst might happen at any moment. My mother could not repress her overprotective behavior towards Joe which, instead of helping him, somehow suffocated him. But, who can accuse a desperate mother for over protecting a child when she sees him falling into a deep abyss?

Joe tried to commit suicide repeatedly, but with each attempt we always arrived in time to save his life and to put him in a treatment program, hoping that it would help him to recover once and for all.

Shortly after I got married I joined the Army. Joe and I didn't see each other for about three years, but after my wife and I returned from Italy, and I was released from my military duties, Joe and I worked together building houses. We became an unstoppable team again as if our strong relationship had never changed. At that time I was responsible for providing for my family and Joe was still a bachelor.

In 1975, my family and I moved to Minnesota to set up our farm there. Life had been very tough for Joe because of all the drugs he had taken. He had been in and out of mental institutions; that didn't help him at all. Most of these places oversimplified treatment with the aid of mind-numbing pills; few actually investigated the reasons why people become drug addicts. They gave pills to the patients, which made the real problem worse. Proper psychological support was rarely available; medication and confinement in isolation seemed to be the mainstay of treatment. Little by little we were losing Joe. We didn't know how to bring him back to his healthy self.

One freezing Winter, Joe was in the woods cutting a tree down for firewood when he had a terrible accident that ended up ruining his life. The tree he tried to cut was frozen, and when he had cut about halfway through, a gust of wind hit the tree and made it split in half. The other half hit him with the force of a furious tempest and permanently disfigured in his face. This was the icing on the cake. Now Joe was burdened with his addiction to drugs, his reliance on medications he received from institutions for the mentally ill, and now *this*. The disfigurement of his face finalized the deterioration of his self-esteem.

Joe attempted suicide multiple times while I lived and farmed with my family in Minnesota. We developed our farm business for 11 years. We stayed there until my wife started missing her side of the family, so we decided to return to Maryland.

When we came back to Maryland, my parents and my brother Joe were very happy to see us again. Joe still retained that glow of the brilliant, enterprising young man, and of the great friend that had always lit him from within. My brother - who was also my best friend - was right there in front of me, yet he was nowhere. His addiction to drugs and the psychiatric medication kept Joe ensnared in a dark nebula where he could not be reached. I imagine that it had also been difficult for him to be able to reconnect with himself.

I did not want Joe to be in a state mental institution, so I paid for him to receive better treatment at a private clinic. I hoped that we were not too late to help him out of his deadly state of mind.

One day, he asked if we would stay in Maryland forever or if would we return to Minnesota. Something in that question made me feel strange, but I could not understand what caused the chill that ran down my spine. I was worried to hear how often my brother talked about suicide, and I spoke with his psychiatrist. The doctor told me that the medication he was taking would prevent Joe from taking his own life.

But that day arrived. The day we dreaded, the day we never wanted to come. What was I doing at that time? What distracted me that I didn't sense it might happen? How was it possible that we could not say goodbye? My brother and best friend was gone, and I felt it the moment my wife told me that my sister was on the phone. She couldn't stop crying and the grief filled her eyes and throat with tears. She could hardly talk but I understood everything. Joe hung himself. I implored heaven that Joe could find the peace he did not have during our terrible childhood as refugees, then as exiles and then later in his very harsh life. My siblings and I have looked for reasons to justify the deep depression that led Joe to take his own life, but we did not find an answer. Not even his psychiatrist could understand why the prescribed medication didn't help Joe overcome the compulsion to kill himself. There was no one to blame, and if there had been someone, nothing and no one would have been able to give Joe back to us.

My mother fell into a deep sadness from which it was difficult to recover. We supported each other as a family. We were and are united in a love that could rise to that heaven where Joe could now be; we prayed that our love would bless him and release him from darkness.

My beloved parents, were my heroes until the end of their long lives. God granted them a serene and long old age. Each lived more than 80 years. Who would have expected such resilience, such longevity, after enduring so much suffering during the Second World War and in the immediate post-war period under the dictator Tito? Yes, our parents inspired us and gave us the courage to endure through the worst and to continue evolving despite the most inhumane treatment. Like those post-World War II victims, we all walked under the impious rage of racism, dictatorship, hunger, and the terrible pain of seeing the innocent die.

8

Where Did the Angel Who Saved My Life Go?

"No, I never saw an angel, but it is irrelevant whether I saw one or not. I feel their presence around me."

Paulo Coelho

In 1966, I purchased a one-acre lot from my parents. My brother Joe and I built a house on that lot. We finished the house a year later. We did a good job and It looked very appealing. My wife and I decided to put it up for sale. I just hoped that those who would live there would be honorable and have good, kind hearts. My brother and I put so much passion, dedication, and love into building that house.

One day a young couple came to the property. They wanted to buy it but the bank didn't approve a loan. I talked to them and looked into their dreams. There was something about the couple that reminded me of the difficult days of my life. I remembered our times in the concentration camps where we, as ethnic Germans, had to experience horrendous inhumane treatment. I also remembered when we were the ragged slaves of some Austrian farmers; we were also subjected to mistreatment by some Austrians who damned us for being refugees.

Yes, that couple was young, with small children and big dreams, and perhaps their lives would one day be blessed as ours had been. I saw that in their eyes. I remembered, too, how many times I would have died if it had not been for the hands of God sending me a guardian angel to rescue me from the misfortune and near death. I also remembered how blessed were my parents, my siblings, our relatives, and the family that I later formed with the beautiful girl with the rotten tomato on her face!

Elisabeth, the same beautiful girl who later became my life partner and the mother of my beloved children. Thinking about all that, and consulting with my wife, we made a fortunate decision for them. It was our way of thanking God for his endless blessings to us all. After talking to my wife we decided to hold the mortgage for that young couple and their children - they had a 20-year mortgage and for 17 years they had always paid on time. We gave them the deed for the house and told them that the mortgage had been paid in full for them which was their Christmas Present from us.

By then I was working as a union carpenter. I built a high school, commercial buildings, bridges, and high-rise buildings. Even though the pay was very good, the work was very dangerous. One unfortunate day I fell 18 feet onto the concrete floor, landing on the side of my head. In the process I bit off my upper lip. I broke a couple of ribs, as well. And, I thanked the strength of my genes and my youth, and sent my gratitude to the guardian angel who prevented the fall from being fatal.

Another near-death experience occurred in North Wilmington. We were putting diesel tanks in. Another carpenter and I were putting in forms for the footings; we were working ten feet below ground. I was on the outside of the form, from the embankment and in a second the embankment crashed down over me and buried me up to my neck. Again, I escaped with my life, after breaking a few more ribs.

At the Dover power plant, I was working on top of a scaffold 117 feet high. I was holding a sheet of plywood to be put on the wall. Just as I was about to nail the plywood to the wall, the crane operator suddenly and unexpectedly raised up a whole skid of plywood, which hit the scaffold halfway up. The next thing I knew was that I was hanging on for dear life to a 2"x8"x8' long scaffold board. It took awhile for me to stop shaking. By the time I got down to ground level, the operator was no longer on his job. If I had fallen 117 feet, I would have died, and still today I wonder what had inspired me to grab that scaffold board which saved my life. The construction foreman told me that the crane operator was drunk when he hit the scaffold with the skid of plywood. After 'receiving' too many close calls, too many hints, to watch out for my life, I made up my mind. I realized that no amount of the money was worth my life. That's when I quit.

In 1971, my wife gave birth to another child, Tony. His sister Santina would carry him on her hip and I would say to my birthday daughter to put him down as he will not walk as long as she kept carrying him around like that. I was still in the Army Reserves at Dover Air Force Base, employed as a civil service worker in a supply warehouse.

Every day there were so many brothers and sisters coming to the Dover Air Force Base receiving wooden boxes - the bodies of their loved ones - from Vietnam. They were coming home to be buried. Don't tell me about the pride of burying a child with honors, trumpets, and a 21-gun salute to the sky. The United

States flag covering the coffins as a symbol of honor and glory was little consolation for the irremediable loss of a son or daughter who lost their lives for dubious reasons that were never worth the sacrifice.

Many survivors of the wartime experience came home loaded down with emotional trauma and addiction to heroin and other drugs that may have been consumed as a result of the terrible horror of bloodshed and war.

I had come a long way from Yugoslavia. I learned about the flashbacks and nightmares suffered by soldiers and civilians; that even when our body breathes, and the heart keeps beating, in some places of our consciousness, there are incurable psychic wounds that we in modern times have labelled 'Post-Traumatic Stress (PTS)'.

It is interesting to see how governments keep influencing young people to join the armed forces to defend the honor of the homeland. Young people take the bait to become heroes of their country, but the reality is that when they return to their homeland many are so psychologically deteriorated that it is very difficult for them to resume a normal life, starting or rejoining a family, and it is often extremely difficult to get a decent job. Not many people want to be 'associated' with the lives of psychologically disturbed individuals, many of whom had sustained permanent psychological damage.

There were days when I felt guilty that I didn't get killed. What comforted me was the thought that there *had* to be a purpose to my life: after all, I had survived all those near encounters with 'lady death' and didn't die.

I know that my questions about *'why, why, why?'* I didn't die in any of the close calls hasn't been answered. Perhaps I didn't die so I could help others who have crossed my path; perhaps I survived to raise my family, or to have the opportunity to share my experiences with you. But seeing the inert bodies of those innocent youth sent home from the war, innocents who were in Vietnam perhaps against their will, made the idea of continuing to work at Dover Air Force Base repugnant to me, and so I quit.

While my wife Elisabeth was working at a facility for chronically ill seniors, I started working for Leed's Travel in Clayton, Delaware. I was installing a big rubber door for forklift operators. Each door was 12' high and 5' wide and weighed 350 pounds. I was up ten feet on an aluminum ladder drilling holes installing a door. As I was doing this, the drill shorted out and I got electrocuted. I could not let go of the drill and I was unable to scream for help. I knew it would just be a matter of seconds before my heart would stop. I looked down and there was a man in a white robe. He had a glow around him. I thought that my vision was getting cloudy or that I was having the experience of approaching death when I saw the halo that surrounded him. He went straight to where the electric cord was plugged in and unplugged it. He then walked in through the opening where I was supposed to install the doors.

After I climbed down the ladder, I immediately went to the opening where the man had just walked through, but I couldn't find him. He was simply not there. I asked the women who worked there if they had seen the man that I described and they said that no one passed by since they were there. When I explained the reason for my question, one of them said that he might have been an angel and I immediately responded, "And then, where did the angel who saved my life go?" All I know is that I was neither dreaming, nor drinking, nor having a hallucinatory experience. I examined the drill. It was burned.

It's hard to provide physical evidence that angels exist. I know

I have my guardian angel and I have other angels, who have been supporting me in times of trouble and life-threatening events.

One day a female friend told me this story when I shared these experiences with her. She had always wondered why some people died crossing the train tracks; why didn't they hear the whistle of the approaching train? Didn't they see the light of the locomotive as it moved toward them along the tracks? But one day her question was answered. She had arrived at a train station in a small town and then set out to cross the tracks by foot. There were several tracks where trains came and went in both directions. "It was around six in the afternoon," she said, "and it was getting dark. I looked everywhere before crossing," she continued, "and I did not see any train. Suddenly, in the middle of the tracks, I heard someone calling my name. I stopped and turned my head to see who had called me, but there was no one there. At that moment, a train passed by at high speed and if I had continued walking, it would have run me over and killed me. I was stupefied. Shocked, but grateful. I wondered where that 'voice' might have come from; the voice had saved my life. It must have been my guardian angel!"

9

Raising Our Family on a Farm

"We must plant the sea and herd its animals using the sea as farmers instead of hunters. That is what civilization is all about - farming replacing hunting."

Jacques Yves Cousteau

When a position for a painter opened at the Dover Air Force military housing I went to work as a painter. I was a Staff Sergeant (E6).

In Washington, DC there is a wall inscribed with the names of 58,000 of my brothers and sisters who had died in Vietnam. I can't go to that Vietnam wall because I want to remember them as if they were still alive.

I was eligible to be promoted to Master Sergeant, but there was no such position available in Dover, Delaware with the 315th S&S Company (DS). Then, in 1975, an opening became available in International Falls, Minnesota with Company B 367 Engr Bn. It was a family vacation time, so we went to see Niagara Falls and Canada. We followed the Canadian border until we arrived at Fort Frances, and then we entered the United States. I looked around the International Falls, Minnesota base and the possibility for a new assignment with the Army Reserve. Our children were very excited about moving there. We went to a real estate agent and purchased 40 acres of land, 14 miles from International Falls and four miles from the town of Ray, Minnesota. My wife and I were raised on a farm and we wanted our children to have the same experience.

There were no buildings on that land.

After we returned to Marydel, Maryland, we left our children with their grandparents and we went back to Minnesota where we purchased the land and built a shed big enough to store our belongings after we moved there. We bought a traveling trailer for us to live in while we built our house. Our parents organized a festive moving party. We departed with wide smiles on our faces and love in our hearts.

My wife drove the pickup with a trailer and I drove the U-Haul truck. It had been raining for a couple of days before we arrived at our new site and we had to cross the railroad tracks to get to our property. Elisabeth led the way driving the pickup with the trailer and she had no problems. When I drove over the railroad tracks I got stuck: the truck had a lot of weight in it. We had to load our belongings onto the pickup truck and drive it to the shed we built earlier. It was about a quarter of a mile from where the U-Haul truck got stuck. We arrived during the first week of June. Our youngest, Tony, was 3 1/2 years old. Ferdinand III was 12, Santina was 11, my wife Elisabeth was 32 and I was 33.

At the very beginning we had no shower in our trailer. I got a 55-gallon drum and put it on top of the shed where we kept our belongings. I put a spray nozzle, ordinarily was used in the kitchen sink to rinse off the dishes, on the bottom of the barrel.

In the morning I put water in the drum so the Sun could warm it up. In the evening the water was warm enough for us to take a shower and it worked great. The only problem with taking a shower outside was the mosquitoes. These were very tiny fleas, so small that they easily got through the screens. When they bite us we could feel it, and each bite left a red spot on the skin. We checked each other for wood ticks and always found them on us.

We had four months to build our new home before the snow arrived. There was an area covering about half an acre which rose four feet above the surrounding land.

That's where we agreed to build our house. I bought one hundred feet of measuring tape to map out the dimensions, used a nail and fastened the beginning of the tape to the ground, then I started walking with it and I said, "You tell me how far to go". It was 70 feet long by 24 feet wide. Then, I got a backhoe and used it to dig out a basement with the same dimensions as the house's perimeter.

From the outside, the house looked like an A-frame house. The house was almost finished by the time it started to rain and snow. We moved to the basement for the Winter and used a barrel stove to heat the space. There was a lot of scrap wood left over and two of our neighbors brought seasoned firewood; normally the firewood has to be stored a year for it to dry. We were living in the basement while we finished the upstairs and stored firewood for the year to come.

I need to backtrack. One night, when I was sitting on the back end of the house with my butt inside of the door and my feet on the outside, I held a flashlight between my legs in the dark and worked on an extension cord that I cut in half. I was splicing it together. It must have been about midnight when I heard a growl and a pig grunting and I said to Elisabeth, "stop trying to scare

me back to bed. I will come as soon as I finish this electric cord."
In the morning, when we were having breakfast, I told her that
she didn't scare me the previous night. She had no idea what I
was talking about. When I explained the sounds she said that it
wasn't her. After breakfast, I went outside and saw bear tracks.
The tracks ended about eight feet from where I had been sitting
on the floor. Thinking back on it, I realized that our German
Shepherd had been barking. He was on a chain.

In the Spring we were all ready and very enthusiastic about
moving upstairs. Everyone got their own room.

Minnesota winters are very challenging compared to winters
in the eastern
part of the United States. It was 40 degrees below zero around
Christmas time and it remained extremely cold until February.
This kind of dry cold weather was the norm for Winter in
International Falls. We learned to have fun during the four
seasons and were very grateful for the life we made. One time
our children wanted to make a snowman; we sprinkled the snow
with water so they could roll the snow. We heated up our home
with a wood stove and had to put water on the stove to keep the
rooms moist; otherwise, we could wake up in the morning with
dry sore throats.

There was so much to learn from our natural surroundings.
So much to learn about dealing with wild animals and with the
cold inclement weather. We bought a Caterpillar D8 bulldozer
equipped with a winch that is used to pull trees. I gathered and
winched them up to the bulldozer, pulling them to the woodshed
after cutting the tree into the length we needed for our woodstove.
It was very easy to split the wood because it was frozen. That's
why everyone makes their firewood in the Winter.

I remember the first time I used the bulldozer, it was about

40 below zero and I just left it on the snow. In the morning, the engine started right up because it had engine block heaters which were plugged into the power. But when I put it in gear to drive it, the engine stalled. It didn't take me long to figure out why it wasn't moving. The tracks from the bulldozer had frozen over. Since then, I parked it on top of the trees that I brought up from the woods to make firewood.

Vehicles, equipment, or whatever we needed to use had to be plugged in. We used to bulldoze our driveway, making a snow-free area for the pickup and the car. Sometimes it snowed more than two feet. When our house was finished, we already had firewood for the Winter to come.

When we lived in Maryland we used to have a garden every year. We decided to plant a garden here, but the soil conditions were very different. The soil was mostly clay, making for a very heavy ground. When it was dry it felt like concrete. The shed we built became the chicken coop where the hens laid their eggs.

My position with Company B 367 Engr Bn active Army reserve at International Falls was supplier sergeant. Sometimes I had to decide whether the person was lying to me or not. When I took over, I found an inventory with many missing items. I reported to the first sergeant that I would not sign off regarding the missing supplies. A retired military person, who worked as acting temporary supply sergeant, informed me that all of those supplies had disappeared while the reserve unit administrator was in charge. It was not my responsibility to find out how they disappeared. I told the first sergeant that I would only sign for what was there at that moment. He agreed with those terms and only the two of us had the keys for the locks.

Our property was mostly in the woods, and we needed grazing land for our livestock. I started on the north side of the chicken coop. There were mostly willows and bushes, and that old bulldozer did a fine job clearing about 15 acres. I pushed all into a row.

While I fed the livestock, away from the chicken coop, I heard the chickens flapping their wings and screaming. I ran over and saw a black bear trying to catch the chickens. Immediately our dog ran out as quickly as he could run. The black bear ran over to where I cut the bushes and the trees into a row, and the bear went into a hole. The dog continued running following the bear.

The dog did not come out of that hole, and I didn't want to go where the black bear was. I walked around on top, yelling, hoping that the dog would come out. I shook the bushes and trees, but nothing happened. My wife came and when she was about two 200 feet from me, I asked her to call the game warden. After a while the game warden, my wife, and our dog appeared. When I saw the dog beside my wife, I wondered how he managed to get into and out of the hole. I realized that the row was about 30 feet wide with a tunnel that went through the other side — and that was how he got out.

We bought 50 pigs, 35 to forty pounds each. We were thrilled with the idea of having farm animals. Among those animals, we had 300 sheep. Sometimes wolves would jump the fence and attacked them. As the wolves were protected we couldn't kill them or prevent them from invading. The government was supposed to pay for the losses but it took a very long time and the amounts we were paid were negligible. On the east side of our property, we had bought from the state 40 acres, all in the woods. After I bulldozed the trees into a row I then cut the smaller trees, which were approximately four inches thick.

I picked up a tree by its roots and extended the length of the tree up to the back windshield then got behind the wheel and started to drive. I turned my head to the back windshield and it suddenly popped out, right over my head and my neck. I wasn't able to turn my head to the front and the tractor was bouncing up and down while I had the windshield tight against my neck. Finally, I managed to pull it out and there was blood all over the cab. I put my gloves on both sides of my neck to slow down the bleeding.

When I got off the tractor I started running home on the field and I was about halfway when I noticed that the pigs were running towards me. I still had about a quarter of a mile to go. The pigs were gaining on me and I ran as fast as I could while holding my neck. There was an electric fence about 200 feet from the house, and I barely made it over the electric fence before the pigs caught up with me. They must have smelled the blood and wanted to attack me.

The sows, gilts, and bores were always allowed to go out to pasture - especially for the breeding season. Every breeding sow, gilt, and bore was identified by ear tags; we had a recorded history of the animal from the time it was born, its performance, history of sickness, and (especially for sows) the number of piglets they had weaned. When the sows were pregnant I was able to judge, just by looking at them, when that sow would have her babies. I would write down the number from their ear tag and that sow was moved into the farrowing house so she could have her babies inside.

I used to drive to Mankato, to pick up a truck loaded with soybean meal from the processing plant and returned home. The roundtrip took more than 21 hours, and I had to go there whether it snowed, the roads had black ice, or the temperature was 50 below zero. While I was gone, my family had to deal with all kinds of problems such as frozen water pipes and electrical problems - just to name a few.

There were five of us in the immediate family, and we knew each other's jobs on the farm and with our animals. We were very supportive of each other. When the children came home from school around 3:30 in the afternoon, they had something to eat and after that, it was time to take care of our animals. We normally finished our chores at about 7:00 pm. During dinner we shared as a family what we had done during the day. Every Saturday we all went out to eat and to watch a movie. Back home we all enjoyed our ice cream dessert.

I used to be a member of the Koochiching County Farm Bureau, which was in charge of policy development concerning farming issues. I lobbied at the state and the national level. The farm families with the Koochiching County Farm Bureau used to order a semi-truck loaded with oranges for their families.

Our farm was the delivery location for the oranges, and we lived next to the Canadian National Railroad tracks. It was Winter and there was a lot of snow. The driver of the semi-truck, loaded with oranges, got stuck on the railroad tracks and he walked to our house and told us what happened. It was one of those 40 below zero nights. The night before I came back with a load of corn and then put back the truck into the shed. I was not planning on unloading the truck for four days. I didn't plug the electrical cord to the block heater on the motor. Still, it started, and I ran to the basement where I kept a chain. I backed up my truck to the semi-truck and hooked them together. My truck began to hammer; I knew what was going to happen. So, I just kept on pulling it off the tracks, and my motor finally seized up. The engine stopped running while the oil came out from the crankshaft bearings. At least I had pulled out the semi-truck and prevented a derailing. What happened was that because the oil hadn't been warmed, the oil pump couldn't pump the oil, and if the crankshaft doesn't receive it, it gets so hot that it burns the bearings. A newer motor would cost us $16,000. I had to decide whether to choose between our savings or safety. I would have to get out of bed at different times to check on guilds to see if we would have problems delivering the piglets.

My wife and I learned from our parents how to make all kinds of cold meat such as sausage, ham, bacon - very well produced charcuterie. Our garden provided us with a wide variety of vegetables which lasted through the freezing winter. From the river that ran alongside our home we caught fish and either smoked them, or with another cooking process put them in jars. We also had a root cellar for our food and, of course, for the wine. Our children learned from us by doing. They learned what my wife had learned from our family back home. We were blessed with an inspiring tradition that taught all of us how to independently sustain our lives.

One beautiful sunny Summer day, I was walking through our woods and came to an area where there was a hazelnut bush. I pushed away the bush and arrived at a meadow, a nice open area surrounded by thick woods. Then I saw a black bear sleeping. It woke up, and we each sized up the other. I didn't move, didn't scream or make noise, as some people suggest to do. The black bear might have sensed my respect, and we both walked off in different directions.

After church, we used to go on Sundays to pick blueberries and mushrooms. Our favorite mushrooms were morels - very delicious. Those moments, sometimes, brought me back to my childhood. I remembered the time (after fleeing from Yugoslavia and living with the farmers who made us slaves) that I went with my mother and siblings to a State Park to gather blueberries and mushrooms when we were starving. The government didn't forbid the people to get things from the State Parks, but it was absolutely forbidden to pick up even one piece of grass from the farmers' fields. These were the same farmers who worked us like slaves, laboring on their farms hour after exhausting hour. So, I used to see with immense joy, how happy my children and wife were picking up nature's gifts from our woods, and I was so thankful for the life that we were now able to live.

My wife would use to bring us a picnic lunch, and we went to our favorite blueberry patch to pick up more. One day a black bear with her cubs was up in the trees where our blueberry haven was. She didn't want us there. The mother black bear sent her cubs further up the tree, then she moved down and started shaking the branches, demanding that we leave her territory. We were not going to argue with the female black bear as it might have been the last thing we would do.

I was also happy to see that our children learned to deal with all kinds of threatening challenges in the wild, because I knew that those experiences would strengthen their character. They grew up without fear, cautious and respectful of all that nature had to offer. It included treating plants and all animals with the same respect we treat all people.

Living in the forest and on the farm was a magnificent life experience for our children who learned, among other things, that even the most dangerous animals would not attack if they did not feel threatened by us. Of course, neither my wife nor I have ever encouraged our children to go out to hunt animals. At an early age, our children learned that kindness, compassion, and respect do not begin or end during Sunday morning sermons. They learned to cultivate these virtues on a daily basis with each person they interacted with; the same attitude applied to how we treated the wild animals, as well. In our way, we were protectionists of the natural world. Maybe that's why, mysteriously, the fiercest animals never attacked us. This gave our children confidence about the importance of observing correct behavior at all times.

The 50 degree below zero temperature didn't reduce the ticks of the woods and there were hundreds of mosquitoes when we went to gather blueberries and mushrooms. We got used to them. The wood ticks were not a big issue either: we put a lot of garlic in our meals and these ticks didn't like the garlic smell coming out from our skins.

After leaving the military, I had more time to spend with my family. We were all very playful and enjoyed our time together very much. My wife was always playing jokes on me like throwing a raw egg at me when I was reading the newspaper or sprinkling water on me from the hose when I was sitting on the porch reading a book or just daydreaming, happily enveloped by the beautiful nature surrounding our home.

On April Fool's Day, she put something on my side of the bed that was a great surprise. Our youngest son Tony, would throw a frozen chicken egg at his brother Freddy and knock him out. Tony and I were sleeping on top of the chicken coup, each in our own sleeping bag next to each other. The temperature was forty below. Tony was making friends in the Catholic school with a shy girl. He was in first grade. Tony wanted to have a Skadu (Austrian) snowmobile, but I said he had to buy an American one. We went to a local John Deere dealer and bought a John Deere snowmobile. A few days later Tony showed me that it was made in Taiwan. Our oldest son Ferdinand (Freddy) threw a piece of dry dirt at me, hitting me on the side of my head while his grandfather stood next to him as I drove the tractor raking hay.

Our daughter, Santina, was carrying a dead chicken and crying. She was afraid: I told them that if the dog killed a chicken again, we would have to give him away to someone who doesn't have chickens.

One April Fool's Day, Santina put vinegar in a glass of water for me to take medicine and I sipped it in one gulp. I spit it out immediately. Everybody was laughing. For the first nine years we had no television. We played games, read books, and did everything together as a family.

Our farm family business kept us very busy. We were mostly raising 40 pound
feeder pigs. We lived in Ray, where no one locked their door. When someone was stranded in a vehicle, they had to find a place to escape from the weather to prevent freezing to death. We have had people while we were not at home come into our house to use the phone and wait until someone came to pick them up. They always left us a 'thank you' note.

The extreme cold would push up rocks the size of four kitchen tables. I would have to dig them out because the plow would gets caught on them and get damaged. After I dug them out, I would pick up those massive boulders with an International Farmall H Tractor which had a narrower front wheel and a manure bucket on the front. Those rocks were so heavy that the hydraulic system barely managed to lift them. The boulders had to be driven to the edge of the woods.

Because of the narrow front on the tractor, driving it with a huge rock on the manure bucket was a real challenge. One time I was driving and turning the front wheels to the right and I hit a hole. The rock shifted to the right inside that bucket. That rock out-weighed the tractor, which turned on its right side, hitting the ground. I could only jump off the tractor on the left side. Narrow front-end tractors were known to flip over on their sides. That happened twice. Also in extreme cold weather, if the tractor had not been plugged into the power, and one needed it right away, the oil in the engine would get so stiff that the engine wasn't able to start. The local people would cover the tractor with a tarp and build a fire under the oil pan to heat the oil.

I needed the tractor after a severe snowstorm. It had snowed about three feet overnight. I needed the tractor so I could feed the animals, which meant pushing the snow from the house, the milling building, nursery, farming house, and control fleeting building. I also had to clear our long driveway so the children could get to the end of the path, where they were picked up by the school bus. So, I did the same thing as the locals did when they heated up the oil on the tractor. On one occasion, I didn't pay attention to the size of the fire; the tractor caught on fire and I had to rewire the electrical system.

One unfortunate day, a relative drove the snowmobile over the main water line.

Our immediate family knew that driving on a water line would cause the frost to come down and freeze the line, which was 15 feet below ground level. The coldest that I remember in the 11 years that we lived there, the temperature plummeted to 56 degrees below zero. That was the Winter they drove over the main water line! We had 1,800 pigs, 10 head of beef, 350 sheep, laying hens, and six goats. The five of us had to carry water with 5-gallon buckets, two buckets each, a distance of approximately 200 feet, twice a day. Almost a thousand gallons in the morning and another thousand gallons in the evening, at temperatures near 45 below zero, wearing much needed wool masks.

We carried water for over a week before we were able to

unfreeze where it had been driven over. After that incident, no one was allowed to drive their snowmobile near the main water line. The house water supply was on a different system and did not affect the house. The 200 amp electric main breaker, which provided electricity for the pig operation, caught fire one day. We needed electricity for grinding feed, electric heat for the nursery, for the farrowing house, and for the ventilation system to prevent methane gas buildup underneath the pits. In freezing weather on a Sunday, I called International Falls Electric Supply, but they did not have a 200 amp electric main breaker panel. The nearest next place was Duluth, and I asked the owner of the Duluth Electrical Supply store if he would open the store and sell me what I needed. It was 156 miles from the farm. It took me about two hours and 20 minutes to get to the electric panel and another two hours and 20 minutes to return to the farm. After coming back to the farm, I removed the old panel and replaced it with the new one, which took another two hours. Most people that operate farms are very resourceful. They have to be. Operating a farm requires to have veterinary, mechanical, and electrical skills. Most of all it takes good common sense!

I took a load of pigs to Fargo, North Dakota, at a time when gasoline was hard to

get. After selling the pigs to J. Morrison in Fargo, the truck was sterilized to ensure that I had not picked up any viruses or bacteria at the stock market. Outside of Fargo, I went to a local elevator and purchased 22 tons of corn before it closed for the day. I was sure that I would have enough gas to drive from Fargo to Badet. When I arrived at Badet at about 11 p.m., all the gas stations were closed, because of the shortage of gas. I looked at the gas gauge: there was 1/8 of a tank left. I knew there was a town called Lohman approximately 35 miles from Badet. I started driving again and it was snowing very hard. I was talking aloud with God saying, "If you want me to get there, please make sure that I don't run out of gas."

As I approached Lohman, the needle on the gas gauge read zero. Lohman had only one gas station. International Falls was 25 miles from Lohman, I said, "Well God if you want me to get to International Falls, you'll have to get me there." I continued driving, relying on my faith, and the needle on the gauge never budged from zero. When I arrived at International Falls, there were four gas stations, and every one of them said, "NO GAS". From there to the farm was another 14 miles. Again, I was talking to God, saying out loud, "Well you brought me this far, so now you have to get me back home."

God did make sure that I got back, at about 2 a.m., with those 22 tons of corn. I told my wife that God had brought me home.

In the morning I was going to drive the truck closer to the milling building to unload the corn. I wanted to start the truck, but no matter how much I tried, it wouldn't start. I put five gallons of gas into the gas tank, turned the ignition to start, and it started right up. After I had unloaded the corn from that small center door, I noticed that there was some corn that was frozen to the corner of the bed of the truck. I unlocked the door on the right-hand side and pulled on the door to open it up, and the top and bottom hinges broke. The door came crashing down, hitting me on my right shoulder. One door alone weighs about 300 pounds. The manufacturer for the straps said that the extreme cold can cause the hinges to snap. I personally believe that God was reminding me who was Boss.

I was operating the bulldozer to make a stock pond for the animals to drink from. It was 50 feet wide by 100 feet long. I had to push out a lot of dirt. I started early in the morning because the weatherman said that it would rain later that evening and I wanted to get it done before the rain. I was operating the bulldozer faster than normal and was about to get everything done when all of a sudden the track on the bulldozer broke in half. The bulldozer and I were nearly on the bottom of the pond.

A broken bulldozer track is not easy to repair. To make matters worse, there was not enough time before the pond would get filled up with rain. I had to find a way to get that bulldozer out of the pond; if the engine got submerged in the water it would be very costly to have it repaired. That D-8 Caterpillar bulldozer weight 52,000 pounds. We brought the truck, which was loaded with 22 tons of grain, then brought a Case Tractor and dug a hole with the loader and backed that tractor into the hole. Later, we brought the International Harvester Tractor and backed it up into the hole. I hooked the grand truck, the Case Tractor, and the International Harvester Tractor together with chains. The winch from the bulldozer was hooked to the grain truck. My wife had her foot on the brake of the grain truck, and the other two had their feet on the tractor breaks. I started the engine on the bulldozer, put the gear in reverse, and pulled the lever on the winch. The bulldozer came right out of that pond while still on the track that had broken in half.

We needed a clear land for our animals, and there was an 80-acre parcel, approximately six miles from our farm, to bid on. The County took care of the elderly person until their death and gave the property to the undertaker for his burial. The undertaker had people bid on that property. All the buildings were very old and in very bad shape; therefore, it was likely that they would be torn down. The buildings were all locked up, so no one knew what was inside. The bid was on an 80-acres parcel of land. The bid I submitted was $ 5,000.01. As soon as the local people found out about my offer they said: "This eastern person paid far too much for the property".

We received the keys to the buildings that required repair. We walked into the house, and my wife and I were surprised to see that the house was filled with old furniture, dating back to 1900 and earlier. In another building, there were other jewels: a 1956 Chevrolet, a 1951 Studebaker, and a McCormick Deering Model F12 made by International Harvester in Rock Island, Illinois in 1936. The International Harvester had front steel wheels, back-steel wheels with spokes, last color red in June of 1936, and after June 1936 that same model tractor was grey. The first thing we did was contact a furniture consultant, and we received more money than we paid for the farm. We gave the 1956 Chevrolet to our son Freddy, and the 1951 Studebaker to our daughter Tina. There was a lot of other antique items. An individual who also submitted a bid wanted to buy the farm from us. We sold the farm to that person for $36,000.00 with the option that we could use that 80-acre land for five years.

10

How Life Could Easily Be Spoiled

"To see the right and not to do it is cowardice."

Confucius

Our daughter Santina, (Tina), was in the 10th grade and they gave her a magazine to read. The name of that magazine was *The Atlantic*. She had to write an essay on contemporary American literature. When she came home she asked me if I would read the article that she had to write about. While I was reading it, my wife noticed that my face became red. I told her that she wouldn't believe what Tina had to write about. The article was about a young man working and having a daydream about having sex with a native American young woman. It described in detail how he and she had oral sex.

When we went to church, we told them about Santina's school assignment. A substitute teacher from the church said that the school's library also had *Playboy* magazines which anyone could check out.

The parents suggested that we call the school to request a

meeting with the school board. During that meeting, they reminded us that the Constitution permitted *Freedom of Speech,* and they did not think there was anything wrong that children had access to these magazines.

A Sports Editor from the local newspaper was there covering the meeting, and somehow found out that I was of German ethnicity. So, later he published in that paper an article about the meeting and described me as a *"Nazi"* and *a book burner.*

The church congregation were outraged by what the Sports Editor wrote as he described how the school board saw nothing wrong about having those magazines in the school library. Our church and other churches from International Falls formed a parent's committee against the school board, and asked me to speak on their behalf. I did ask the school board for a second meeting, but they were reluctant to do it.

The election for the new school board members was coming up, so finally they decided to meet with us. The State Television News Media came to the meeting, and their opinion didn't differ much from the local newspaper.

At another meeting, there was a church preacher that said that he allowed his children to read whatever they wanted and they were in the third and fourth grades. The parents who attended that meeting booed the preacher and his congregation asked him to leave the church. This situation went on for a year. Towards the end of so many meetings, the TV Media, the local Newspaper, and a local veterinarian said to me, "Mr. Fueller, there is no absolute right or wrong."

I asked if I could approach the school board. When permission was granted, I walked up to the veterinarian and said, "Let's pretend that my hand with the index finger pointing at your forehead is a .45 pistol and I pull the trigger and kill you. Would that be right or wrong?" Everyone in that building applauded for a long time. The International Falls schools had formed a committee led by parents and teachers to read all the books and magazines *before* they entered the school library. Since then, and secretly, *Playboy, Playgirl, The Atlantic,* and sex magazines have been removed from the school libraries.

We had two truckloads of wheat delivered to the farm from a grain *elevator* in Badet. The grain was added to corn-soybean meal and a premixed formula to feed the animals. I noticed that the sows and boars were eating clay. That wasn't normal. I asked the veterinarian to come to our farm, and he said that they behave as if they were trying to put out a fire. He suggested that I should inform the state agriculture representative. The representative came and told me that there was something definitely wrong with the wheat from the Badet *elevator.* I spoke to the supplier in charge of the wheat who said that there was nothing wrong with it. So, the state agriculture representative asked me to fill four burlap bags full of the contaminated grain and request that the grain be tested. I called the *elevator* to pick up the wheat; they kept insisting that nothing was wrong with it. A bag with the contaminated wheat was sent to the University of Minnesota for toxicity testing. The other bags were sent to the University of North Dakota for testing on pregnant sows. The North Dakota's veterinarian said the animals had ulcers in their stomach. The results from the University of Minnesota were also positive, demonstrating high levels of toxicity in the wheat.

We were told to find a lawyer and sue the *elevator.* It was not easy to find a lawyer, because the *elevators* belong to the Elevator Association and suing them would have been almost impossible. There had been complaints from other farmers against that specific *elevator.* Being a member of the Farm Bureau, and being on the Policy Development Committee, I got to know some of the senators and representatives from the state of Minnesota.

There was a senator from Duluth, whose nephew just finished law school. The senator said that he would ask him to represent me. The young attorney brought suit against the *elevator* on our behalf.

While I was waiting to find out when the trial would take place, I went to work for the Department of the Interior, Voyager National Park Service headquarters in International Falls. I worked there as a supply clerk, and it was a very challenging job because I was ordering supplies for whatever the Park needed. I was responsible for effectively meeting those requirements.

The game biologist supposedly lost the $3,000 camera which I had recently ordered for them. There was another person who approved Park supplies and requirements; my signature was also required for approval. That other person approved a request for building floating docks and had ordered $12,000.00 in materials without my consent. He didn't even bother asking the foreman who was in charge of building the floating docks what materials he needed. He ended up with the wrong materials for the floating docks and tried to cover up. The merchant asked for a 20% return on the material policy, and it wasn't ever returned. Then, another supply clerk transferred $12,000.00 from labor money to cover his butt. I told him that he could not legally do that because President Ronald Reagan had allocated that money for labor; now someone would get laid off earlier.

President Reagan had created temporary work with the Park Service and sent a budgeted amount of money for labor, and another amount for materials. I let the Park Superintendent know what was happening. He told me not to worry about it and asked me to be sure that all departments ordered what they needed before the end of the year; the intent was to increase the budget for whatever the Park might need. Then, the Assistant Superintendent asked me to come to her office. After inviting me to sit down, she said that she heard about my conversation with the Superintendent. Lying spread eagle on her chair, she then exposed herself. She didn't have any panties on. She invited me to join her that weekend on a trip to Kettle Falls. I felt insulted and angry. "I don't think so," I said. "I am happily married, and your husband is a friend of mine. Right now at this moment he is downstairs in the store." She felt offended and told me to get out. The person who had improperly transferred that $12,000.00 went with her to Kettle Falls and to Voyageurs National Park, a hotel on an island near the Canadian border, a getaway for politicians and women who provide services for them.

When a position opened up for maintenance, I took it. They were building floating docks on the island in Voyageurs National Park, with a great deal of illegitimate money. There were new snow machines, new boats, and speedometer hanky-panky to bring up mileage on the Park's maintenance vehicles to enable the theft of gas.

Since I was still a member of the Farm Bureau, I told its president how our taxes had been spent. At one of our Farm Bureau monthly meetings, attended by two state senators I spoke about what was happening at Voyageurs National Park. Both of the senators were shocked and responded that they would look into it. They must have looked into it: why else was I was laid off?

Three years had passed since the contaminated wheat put us out of the pig business. It was time to go to court in Badet, about 73 miles from our home. The trial lasted seven days. During that time the first person that testified on our behalf was a professor

93

from the University of Minnesota. He told the jury the name of the toxic elements and the quantity of the poisonous wheat that had been mixed with non-toxic wheat. He also said that the toxicity level was so high that it severely harmed our pregnant pigs to the point where we needed to kill them. On the second day, another professor also testified on our behalf from the University of North Dakota Agriculture Department. He told the court that the contaminated wheat had been given to the pregnant pigs, many of which became intoxicated as a result. My attorney had four *elevator* employees on the witness stand, and he asked them if they knew that there was contaminated wheat added to the uncontaminated wheat. The secretary from the grain *elevator* told the attorneys representing the grain *elevator* that I had not notified the grain *elevator* immediately of any problems with the wheat since I reported it a week later. Their attorney added that if I had notified the grain *elevator* right away, the problem would have been prevented.

We noticed the jury reaction to the statement "it could have been prevented". My attorney became very nervous and said, "We might lose this case". I told him that I could prove that I called as soon as I saw my pigs eating the clay. I could also prove that I had called the grain *elevator* right away. My phone bills documented all my long distance calls to Badet. My attorney requested a recess until the following morning and the Judge agreed.

I went home and looked for the boxes where we kept the phone bills. When my attorney had the proof of my calls in his hand, he again asked the secretary if I called right away and she insisted "No, I had called a week later". Then, my attorney showed her the phone bills. The jurors now knew she lied on the witness stand.

The grain *elevator*'s attorney asked the Judge if he could speak to my attorney in private. He responded that if my attorney accepted, it would be all right. When my attorney returned, he told me that they wanted to make a deal and not continue with the trial. I replied to him loudly, "Absolutely not!"

When the jury returned and gave their verdict that the grain *elevator* was responsible in all counts, and we were awarded a certain amount of money and punitive damages. After the trial was over, the foreman of the jurors came to me and asked me if I recognized him. I responded that I didn't. He said three years ago he had a meeting with the State Police in Duluth, and that he is now with the State Police in Badet. He continued telling me that when he ran out of gas not far from where I lived, he came to me and asked whether I had any gas and I responded that I didn't, but I offered to give him a ride to the next gas station. He also told me that he and other farmers had pigs that suffered the same contamination.

When we won our case against the grain *elevator*, the insurance company for the *elevator,* Aetna Insurance Company, appealed the case and would not pay us. They appealed two more times.

Our attorney, who would receive a percentage from us, did not get paid either. As a senator was his uncle, he asked him for help; the senator subsequently asked the state legislators to pass a law that Aetna Insurance Company could not sell any insurance policies in the state of Minnesota until they paid us for our losses. The Judge that handled our case increased the punitive damages against Aetna. A few weeks later we finally received payment for our losses. We were the first to ever win a lawsuit against a grain *elevator* in the state of Minnesota.

After my daughter Tina asked me to read the article for contemporary American literature, and following what happened in the meeting with the school board the previous year, our church decided to build a new church and a new school. Our daughter had one more year left of high school, which she finished in the new school created by the church. Tony was going to a Catholic school in International Falls at that time, and after the completion of the new school, he also went there.

Our oldest son Ferdinand III (Freddy) joined the Army, about a year and a half before Tina's graduation. Freddy was stationed in Germany. Then, my wife, Tina, Tony, and I went to visit our son Freddy, and when we were all together as a family, we went to visit our relatives in Germany and Austria. Freddy had less than six months left of his two years of commitment to the Army, and after that, he received an honorable discharge and came home.

Tina and Freddy went to the same university in South Carolina. Tina studied education to become a teacher, and Freddy became a preacher. When they came home for the Christmas holidays, they had a friend from Australia attending the same school, and they arrived together. The young lady friend from Australia was a farmer's daughter, and we had a great deal in common. They went all together to get a tree for Christmas, and in spite of the heavy snowstorm they got a magnificent one. The Australian girl had so much fun in the snow with my children that she was laughing all the time. They were laying together in the snow, making snow angels.

I remember one occasion involving my daughter-in-law, a city girl who was then dating my oldest son Freddy. It was Winter, and we had a trench that was between six to eight feet wide. The farrowing house was placed there, and she wanted to see how the sow had their babies, but she couldn't stay because of the smell from the methane gas. So, she came out from there and was leaning against the wall of a snow trench with our Saint

Bernard dog straddling her and licking her face. She kept saying to our dog: "get away from me." I didn't like her angry tone. I told her that if she married my son, our dog was also an honorable member of our family whom we all loved and respected very much; our dog would be part of your marriage.

Some 30 years later she reminds me of that every now and then, reminds me of our precious family moments. I understood then how difficult it might be for a city girl to adapt herself to the life style on a farm. What for us was motivation, entertainment, and the fun of overcoming challenges could be overwhelming to her. But, fortunately, love makes miracles, and she and Tony were made for each other. Love was the necessary glue to keep them united, happy, and always wanting to grow *in tandem*. I doubted that the relationship between Freddy and the city girl would work out in view of their difference but I was overjoyed to be wrong. But my assumptions were rigged, and I was happy that I was wrong. I once heard someone saying something that I found particularly wise and inspiring: "Where there is a will, there is a way".

When the hunting season arrived, I saw one day on the edge of the woods two little deer, furry white spots and all - babies who had lost their mother to a hunter. When I saw the helpless deer babies, unable to get their own food, I decided to feed them. They would not survive the harsh Winter otherwise. Every day I would feed them with my own nutritious formula made by soybean, ground corn, dry milk, salt mineral, powdered vitamins, and a couple of apples. I would mix these ingredients together with some hay. They were receiving their food at a quarter of a mile from our house and as the snow was getting heavy and I brought them closer to the house.

By springtime, I knew that those two were stags and they would co-exist with the farm animals. One day a friend of mine came, and he was surprised that they came right to us, like puppies. I told him what had happened and how I fed them during the entire Winter, and they could come and go as they pleased.

11

The Still Unsolved Mysteries of Life

*"Mystery creates wonder and wonder
is the basis of man's desire to understand."*

Neil Armstrong

Sometimes I had the feeling that someone was following me. Perhaps it was as a consequence of accumulated psychological trauma I buried very deep inside my unconscious mind. The damage might have started when I was in my mother's womb and she wanted to abort me. My living presence, growing in her young body, must have only brought her the painful memories of being raped. I also knew that I hadn't been able to completely heal myself after those years of fear, despair, sadness, and all the persecutions experienced during the different dreadful wars I had been exposed to. All this in spite of feeling happy and very blessed with the family, my wife and I were able to create. And then there was the time I was sent to Vietnam against my will, a bizarre experience I only recall during my recurrent nightmares. Why the persistent feeling that someone was following me?

As a child, I would lie in bed and feel that something was holding me down. Whoever or whatever it might have been it was sucking on my nipples. I couldn't move or even scream. When I was finally able to get up, my nipples were hurting and bleeding. This had been happening for months, and I didn't know what to do or how to explain it.

One day I couldn't bear it anymore. The inexplicable frightened me. I decided to tell my mother about these horrendous episodes. She didn't say anything. She just relied on her wisdom and put a cross above my bed - a cross that had been blessed with Holy Water and her prayers. It never happened again.

International Falls is perhaps, one of the coldest places in America. Winter temperatures reach lower than 50 below zero. The ground crunched when I walked on the frozen snow, and I would see my shadow at two o'clock in the morning.

The stars seemed to be so close that I thought they were jewels hanging from the sky. I thought I could reach them by merely extending my hand. The air was so clean that each breath was capable of purifying my mind and spirit. Maybe my European genes and background enabled me not only to survive but also to enjoy this challenging weather.

A friend of ours came to our home at three in the morning from work and said that on his way to our place he saw a flying saucer at the top of the railroad tracks across from our house. I went and looked. I saw that the snow melted about 40 feet in a circle. I remember reading and hearing about all kinds of mysterious and inexplicable phenomena some might call unidentified flying objects (UFOs). In those days we were so busy with our farm and family that even if I wanted to, I would haven't been able to find the time to explore the hints of enigmatic visitors from somewhere else in the Universe.

I loved walking in our woods in Winter. On one occasion there was a timber wolf that caught a snowshoe rabbit. I immediately screamed at it and ran over to where the lifeless rabbit was. I picked it up by the ears and walked away. The wolf followed me. When I stopped, the wolf stopped too. I walked and he followed. I stopped, he stopped. I was thrilled to see his perseverant behavior. After I played with the wolf walking and stopping, I decided he had earned the rabbit. I left the dead rabbit on the ground and continued walking. The wolf went and picked up his prey, looked at me and trotted away with the booty in his mouth.

The weather where we lived was indescribably cold. Polar bear weather. I knew how it must feel coming very close to freezing to death.

After delivering a load of pigs to the market in Saint Paul, I ran out of gas. This was strange, since I usually kept enough gas for a round trip. The temperature at that moment was 56 below zero, and I was on Interstate Highway 35. No one was on the road; it was 3:30 in the morning. I had the emergency lights on, but they were hardly blinking.

I was already falling asleep when someone's voice woke me up. He was standing on top of a snowbank eight feet high and screaming that someone was on the way, someone who would be there in five minutes. When the tow truck arrived, I was shaking and shivering so bad that I could not talk. I couldn't find the person who had been standing on the snowbank. His voice and presence were not hallucinations. I have no explanation for that experience — he must have been an angel! After the tow truck driver filled the gas tank of my truck, he told me that when the temperature goes so deep down the gas doesn't evaporate. That's why the gas runs out of the tailpipe. I still had about 130 miles to go, and I was still shivering and thinking about the man or the 'spiritual presence' who woke me up and then disappeared. It would have been very dangerous for me to fall asleep in such low temperature I would say that 'he' or whatever that presence was, had definitely saved my life.

A few days later I went snowmobiling. It was late in the evening, and there was a full moon with plenty of stars shining around like infinitely distant diamonds sparks in the clear sky. The moon illuminated the field so well that I could see my shadow. I felt how the moon's powerful strength lit up the night with a magical and mysterious presence. We had a long snowmobile trail that went into our woods and a turnabout where one could return to the same path.

On my way back, I had to stop because there was a female deer head laying on the road. I looked around, and I didn't see any deer tracks. Its head was frozen and the bottom of the severed neck was shining like a mirror, smooth and flat. It looked like it had fallen from the sky. I felt chills. A scary feeling, somehow creepy, the hair stood up on my neck.

There were times during those very crispy and cold nights when I would simply walk. Sometimes I noticed a shadow that wasn't mine, but seemed to belong to someone or something else. I never did find out what it was, but I distinctly remember that it wasn't a frightening presence. I do not know anything about spirits or ghosts. Nor can I say that I have had any experience with alien presence or with visits from extraterrestrials. I have heard about these phenomena and I do not question them because they may well exist. Something I do know is that none of the traumatic situations that I ever lived through weakened the warrior spirit, the spirit that had always been inspired by faith and a refusal to react to challenges with resentment or bitterness.

The day I threw the rotten tomato, at the girl who later became my wife, held an omen. She threw another one at me and that's when our dialogue began. An unusual first meeting that became the beautiful family we were blessed to have. Like all couples, we had our awkward moments, but they only served to strengthen our relationship.

On those cold nights on my lonely walks, I would reflect on what life had given me, and I saw how much good I had received even from the difficult times. I can proudly say that this *unwanted child*, who almost perished so many times as a newborn, as a child, and as an adult, went on to become a father of magnificent children. I have loved my wife unconditionally since the day of the splattered tomatoes.

Yes, the nights used to put me in tune with the book of my life, with the acoustics of my thoughts, and with the thoughts I had heard from my mother, my father, and our ancestors. I sometimes wondered if our thoughts, formed by the electrical relays of our neurons, could create waves, like the waves that a radio emits, like music? Could the thought waves create forms in space and time? Was that the origin of my dream recall of Vietnam?

12

Irreplaceable Memories

"Take care of all your memories. For you cannot relive them."

Bob Dylan

Tony and I were cleaning the building we used to house our pregnant sows and pregnant guilds when suddenly I smelled a non-familiar odor, an odor of smoke. I looked out the door and saw that it was coming from the bottom of the basement door and also from the deck that was connected to the living room. When I went up to the top of the deck and opened the door, a ball of fire and smoke blew me away. Good thing it blew me away, because if I had entered into the room, I would have fallen to the basement and into the fire. I was wearing canvas coveralls, winter clothes and a stocking hat that caught on fire. I had to pull it off right away; in the process it burned off my eyebrows and made my mustache catch on fire. I immediately called the Fire Department from the office I had in the nursery and they arrived about 30 minutes later. They said that the only thing they could do was to make sure that the fire wouldn't spread any further.

In spite of all our efforts, our home became a total loss. It was tough for all of us. We built that house with our own hands; there were so many memories building it, and many more from all the days we lived there together. Although we could have replaced all the material things, we mourned those that were irreplaceable; they were lost forever! Among those irreplaceable losses were films: movies of our wedding day, our children growing up, birthday parties, our trip to Hershey Park, the days we camped in tents, went fishing and crabbing, me in my military uniform, and all of us laughing and crying on special occasions. All of those memories on film and photos could never be replaced. It hurt.

Supposedly, learned in the military to be unbreakable. Let me tell you that the loss of those memories was the hardest thing I ever had to deal with in my life. Photos that have been given to us by our families can't compare to the films that showed the family in sound and movement - as if perpetuated in a timeless moment of doing funny things, crying, laughing, acting silly. Yes, I have built quite a few homes but this wasn't the same. The Minnesota home was priceless because we worked together as a family to build it during all kind of challenging weather: during the heat, and the cold, in the rain, and the snow. We created that house together, built it with dreams, hopes, laughter, dedication, and sacrifice.

The house was insured. At least we received material compensation for the drastic loss. We needed a new place right away, a place where we could live. My wife and I agreed on a three bedroom mobile home trailer and drove to Duluth, about 156 miles from our farm. It was worth the trip. Duluth was a big city and had many mobile home trailer dealers to choose from. We needed many other things as well. The trailer was supposed to be a temporary solution until we rebuilt another home again.

Fortunately, our children Ferdinand (Freddy) and Santina (Tina), were not far from Bob Jones University of Greenville, South Carolina, which is a Christian university.

In those days, my wife occasionally mentioned that it might be the time to return to Maryland. I knew then how much she missed her parents and her siblings. Often she became homesick.

Since we had no more domestic animals on the farm and I had been laid off from Voyageurs National Park, I said to my wife, "Fine, let's go back to Maryland and see if we could find a place and have a business." My only condition was that we would not sell the farm right away.

There was a woman we knew from the church. She and her family were looking for a place to live. We allowed them to stay on our land. All they had to do while living on our farm was to let us know if anything got damaged, for whatever reason. They were staying in a trailer.

We finally found a place in Marydel, Maryland that had a three-bedroom apartment on one side of the building. The other side of the same building had a grocery store. When I first came to America, I lived at a dairy farm not far from that grocery store. I bought my favorite cream soda there; by then I was over 15 years old. An old saying came to my mind about what that happened: *'You never know where life will take you.'*

13

Someone to Watch Over Them

"My father had many, many veterans over to the house, and the older I got the more I appreciated their sacrifice."

Steven Spielberg

I remembered my days in the military and also those when I was living as a young refugee. I thought about how fortunate I was, surviving all those moments when my life hung in the balance. I thought about the beautiful love of my wife. Long ago I heard a song composed by George Gershwin called: *"Someone to Watch Over Me,"* that song came to mind, as well. I thought about the veterans who came back from war with so much disability and suffering. I thought that one day the time would come to help the unfortunate by giving back some of the blessings I received in my life - "to become someone to watch over them." This thought occurred to me when we started living in Marydel.

There was a distant family relative who was a caretaker for military veterans at the Veterans Administration. Before we moved to Minnesota my wife used to work for the chronically ill in Delaware and she had extensive experience working with seniors. We wanted to support the military veterans, too, so we contacted the Veteran Administration about the possibility of caring for military veterans - a program was part of a community residence program. The social workers from the Veterans Administration collaborated with the program and were in charge. Everything had to be approved by the social workers. The Fire Departments made sure that all the security regulations that would provide safe care to the veterans were followed: the rooms had to be a certain size, and smoke and carbon monoxide detectors had to be installed. The fire alarm system had to be operative, and the two evacuation exits had to be approved by the Veteran Administration and the local Fire Department; the plans had to be approved before construction began.

We did the work ourselves. It took us approximately a month to make it ready; after everything was finished, we got the approval of the social workers and the Fire Department. If my wife had not had competent experience working for the chronically ill of Delaware, she would have had to get additional training. We were able to support the veterans right away. We both enjoyed this work very much. It wasn't only a matter of providing appropriate assistance but of providing humanitarian care in a nurturing environment where the veterans' emotional needs could be somehow met as well.

The veterans hospital had developed a program to essentially assist those veterans with mental and/or physical disabilities. My wife and I were responsible for providing anything that the veteran might need help with. The veterans to whom we were responsible for came from a veteran hospital for the mentally ill. We also had to provide transportation for their appointments at different health care facilities. My wife and I started taking care of our disabled veterans by bringing them to restaurants, taking them on day trips, and sometimes providing them an overnight stay at motels if they needed to stay longer.

At first, the Veterans Administration didn't authorize the veterans' trips to restaurants and other places. We were very uncomfortable with the fact that they had to sit around all day doing nothing or sleep in their rooms all day. We wanted them to be able to receive entertainment, to interact with each other and with the people who cared for their needs.

Whenever I had a problem with the Veteran Administration, I would call a senator from Maryland and she would make sure that the veteran received the care that would contribute to the improvement of his quality of life. Of course, these initiatives put me on a list that no one would like to be on. I didn't care what the Veteran Administration thought of me. I was also a veteran and I had first-hand experience of the source of their suffering and despair.

There was a veteran who could not see to walk. He needed cataract surgery. At the next appointment with the psychiatrist, I told the doctor that the veteran needed cataract surgery. The psychiatrist replied, "People like him do not need cataract surgery." I reacted immediately. I asked, "What did you just say? Can you repeat that please?" And he repeated himself: *people like him do not need cataract surgery*. We immediately went to the admission desk and I requested to speak to the hospital administrator. After waiting and waiting, I was allowed to see him and then he contacted the cold-hearted psychiatrist. Unfortunately, after speaking with the psychiatrist, the hospital administrator agreed with his decision. When I returned home, I called the Maryland senator to tell her what had happened and two days later, the veteran received his cataract surgery at the

Veterans' Administration hospital in Wilmington, Delaware. His vision problems were resolved.

We had two veteran homes and we received additional support from our oldest son, his wife, and daughter. They also went to the churches for their ministry in Virginia.

I bought a 23-acre plot with the idea of building a 70 room house with necessary accommodations for the staff. The plans were sent to the Environmental Health Department, to the Planning Board, and the Zoning Board. The Director of the Environmental Health Department did not approve the plans. According to him, a central septic system or central water supply would not be allowed there. For the project, I built a road to the property; the Director of the Department of Environmental Health said that I was not authorized to build a road on the property.

Even though the project had been examined by a certified company in Maryland, we did not get the support of the various governmental agencies. The various agencies fined me $ 10,000.00 each, amounting to a total of $ 50,000 per day. The Director of the Department of Environmental Health had spoken to those different agencies and obviously manipulated them.

Once. we obtained a lawyer, the US Army Corps of Engineers, the Department of Fisheries and Hunting, and the Planning and Zoning Department of Caroline County sent informed us that they did not have the authority to penalize us as there had been no violations.

The Director of the Department of Environmental Health from Caroline County, Maryland, came out to the site accompanied by a person who was from headquarters. I told them that I worked for the Department of Interior as a public servant, so there were also public servants involved. The Director of the

Caroline County Health Department said that he was not a public servant but a public official. I immediately pointed out it was the taxpayers who paid his salary, and that made him a public servant.

The Director from the Caroline County Health Department measured the water table at 30 pipes at 15 different locations on the 23-acre parcel of land. His water table measurements were always higher than ours. He insisted that he was right and he started harassing us. We then hired three different certified companies to take the measurements; none of these companies were affiliated with each other so they couldn't access each other's data. One of those three companies trained the Director of the Caroline County Health Department to measure water tables and to test soil.

We appealed the decision of the Carolina County Health Department to its Health Officer. Three different companies that were doing the water table testing were asked to attend the hearing. The company that had trained the director on water table and soil testing asked the Caroline County Health Officer how one could legitimately rule on this matter when there was friendship between one party and the director of the Environmental Health Department. The Caroline County Health Officer would not allow those three companies to testify on our behalf. We received a letter from Caroline Conley, Health officer. As we expected, Conley ruled in favor of the Director of Environmental Health. The Department of Environmental Health in the state of Maryland was so corrupt that they would not approve percolation tests the first time an application was submitted, and then told the applicants to resubmit the following year, when it was finally passed. They were required to testify before state legislators. The night before testifying, one person jumped off the bridge and the other person killed himself.

The Director of the Caroline County Health Department had approved a housing development for a doctor, his son-in-law, the Director of Planning and Zoning and for a local housing builder.

After they had approved building lots by the Director of the Caroline County Health Department, there was a moratorium which stopped percolation tests and further applications for building lots. At the last public meeting, I testified that they didn't care about what the people said and they held the moratorium so that no percolation testing and building lots applications would be approved. I also said that they essentially decided not to listen to the people, which was very reminiscent of the country that we fled as refugees from a communist dictator. The audience applauded and shouted to the Director of Planning and Zoning: "You are not listening to the people!"

The Director of Planning and Zoning said that he was offended by what I had said and added that this was not a communist country. Someone in the crowd shouted at the Director: "It was exactly what you did!"

The 70 room nursing home for the veterans was at a standstill. I kept thinking about how I could move it forward.

It had been raining for the last couple of days. I said to myself, *I wonder how the septic systems of housing developments (already) approved by the Department of Environmental Health could be approved if there was any water on top of those septic systems.* I got my movie camera and went to the septic systems that had been passed by the Director of the Environmental Health Department. The Environmental Health Housing Development septic systems were underwater; the septic systems of a local home builder was under water too. After I filmed those two locations, I sent the film to the Maryland Attorney General's office.

The attorney we had wasn't able to move forward with the 70 room veterans home. He referred us to a law firm he recommended and we followed his advice. The new attorney was the Assistant Attorney General of Maryland, and was familiar with our case and aware of the film that I sent to the Attorney General's office. He belonged to a very large legal firm and was in touch with the Attorney General. Therefore, he was able to arrange a meeting with the Attorney General who was very concerned about what the Director of the Caroline County Environmental Health Department had done to us, and demanded that a meeting with State Environmental Health had to take place right away.

The Attorney General, our new attorney, the director of State Environmental Health, my wife, my son, and I attended that meeting. The Director of Environmental Health said that he wasn't aware that this had happened to the Fuellers; our new attorney said that our previous attorney had written letters to the State Environmental Health Department and that he had copies of the letters that had been sent to him. The Attorney General said to the Director of Environmental Health Department that what had happened to the Fuellers had to be resolved immediately.

After the meeting, the Attorney General came to me and asked, "Fred, you sent that film to me, with their septic systems being underwater?" I replied, "Yes, I did that!"

To which, he responded that although what I had done wasn't legal, if I hadn't sent him that film, he probably would not have believed me.

A week after the meeting with the Attorney General, we received a letter from the Director of the State Environmental Health Department saying that the Director of the Caroline

County Environmental Health Department had no right to disapprove the central septic system and the central water system for the 70 room home. We re- submitted the application for the central septic system and central water system to the State Environmental Health Department; we were told that that it would be approved, and that it would one to two years before construction could begin. It had been six years since the applications were submitted to the Director of the Caroline County Environmental Health Department. Six years and $48,000 in attorney fees. The Director of the Caroline County Environmental Health Department was removed from his position and did not get state retirement. The Director of the Caroline County Planning and Zoning was also relieved from her position and did not get retirement from the County, either. The problem with opposing employees who work for federal, state, and county agencies is that their attorneys are paid from public tax money. . . and public tax money never runs out.

14

Almost Dying at the Hands of Bad Practices

"A hospital is no place to be sick."

Samuel Goldwyn

Throughout my life. I have heard stories of people who did not want to die in a hospital. I have also heard stories of patients whose chances of survival were greater outside a hospital than in. It is difficult to help someone who is struggling with a disease and all its related stress. That person is treated by a large number of medical assistants, doctors, and nurses, detached from the true needs of their patients.

During all the time we had our businesses, I was receiving health care from the Veterans Administration, and I had been hospitalized different times at different places.

In the beginning, even though a veteran, I was not eligible for dental care. Instead, I went to a local dentist to have a molar tooth pulled out. The dentist injected novocaine in my gums which made my heart race, so they had to immediately take me to Loch Raven Veterans' Hospital. I stayed there overnight, and by the next morning I was okay, and they released me from the hospital.

Several months later, I had a physical and my primary physician scheduled me for an angiogram at Loch Raven. During the procedure, I had chest pain and pain in my left shoulder. The person watching the monitor told the doctor to stop the procedure; otherwise I would have a heart attack. The doctor ignored him. The next thing I knew was that I had been transferred to the University Hospital in Baltimore. My heart condition had been stabilized - something the doctor at Loch Raven Veterans Hospital could not do. After a few days at the University Hospital, I was released and sent home.

A month later they told me to go back to Loch Raven VA Hospital to have the angiogram. Unfortunately, the same doctor was scheduled to do the procedure; again, I experienced chest pain. It was hard to breathe, and once again I had pain in my left shoulder. The same assistant that was on the monitor the last time told the doctor that he needed to pull it out or I might have another heart attack. The doctor replied that I was just a crybaby. The next thing I remember was waking up at the University Hospital to have my heart stabilized again because that same doctor at Loch Raven didn't do it.

Like a recurrent nightmare, a doctor asked me to have the angiogram done again but this time with a different doctor at Loch Raven. When I went back to the hospital they told me that the doctor who was supposed to do the angiogram did not show up. Therefore, the one I had twice before would be doing it, and the nurse asked me to take some pills. Of course, I immediately said, "I am not going to take the pills, and I won't have the angiogram done by the same doctor whose negligence cost me two heart attacks in two months". The nurse didn't want to listen to my reasons, and she insisted that I take the pills. I walked away from her, found a telephone and called my wife; by that time, hospital security were surrounding me, and I told them that my wife was coming to the hospital to pick me up.

I heard from other veterans that down in the basement there were rows of containers with human bodies in them, some without their organs, lungs, legs, or hands. We immediately requested that the angiogram was done in a private hospital. I wasn't going to risk my life under the same doctor who would provoke another heart attack, or even kill me. All I could think about were the containers in the basement with the bodies in them.

To prevent more heart attacks, my primary physician from the Veteran's Administration prescribed pills to thin my blood. But a week later I got mini-strokes and she prescribed one more pill. Two days after taking the extra blood thinner, I had a severe stroke that dropped me down on my knees. I knew right away that I was having a stroke. While I was on my knees, my vision became double, and it took all of my strength to prevent falling over; it seemed like it took a long time for me to convince my mind to keep me alive. About five minutes or so, my vision started clearing up, and I was able to get up on my feet. All this happened when I was at the housing development, three-quarters of a mile from my house. When I got home, I told my wife what had happened.

A woman who worked at the Post Office told me that her father died from a major stroke; he had also been a veteran. I called a private doctor and told him what had happened to me, and he wanted to know the name of the physician from the VA clinic who gave me the extra pill, and the name of the medication that she had prescribed. He asked me not to take another pill because it causes the brain to bleed. The woman from the Post Office said that her father took the same blood thinner which eventually killed him.

In 2003 I was in Yuma, Arizona, for the Winter and when I awoke in the morning, I couldn't see anything from my right eye. I rushed to the Southwestern Eye Clinic. The ophthalmologist took a needle, trying to relieve the blockage of fluid in my eye in the hope that it had done no damage to the optic nerve. He said that usually if the blockage lasted for more than 45 minutes, I would probably lose my vision.

There was a shuttle leaving from the clinic in Yuma to Tucson Veterans Hospital in Arizona. The doctor in that hospital told me that he reviewed my medical record at the Veterans Hospital in Baltimore and said, "I read your medical record. Tell the doctor at the V.A. in Baltimore that you are not able to concentrate well, and that your head is not feeling right."

The doctor in Baltimore ordered an ultrasound of my carotid arteries. The ultrasound showed no obstruction in either of the carotid arteries. The Veteran's Hospital in Tucson showed that a blockage of 90% in the right carotid area, which was coming loose, and a 70% blockage in the left carotid. This explained the loss of sight in my right eye. The person who did the ultrasound at the Veterans Hospital in Baltimore did not know how to do that ultrasound;there was no possibility that the blockages had developed in less than four months. The doctor in Tucson also said that I couldn't sue the Veteran Administration for the loss of my sight. Because of the loss of vision in my right eye, I decided to return to Maryland. Before leaving Arizona, the doctor from the Veteran Hospital in Tucson said that once I get back home, I should go to the Veterans Hospital to remove the 70% blockage in my left carotid artery.

I went to a Veterans Hospital in Wilmington. Delaware and told them what the doctor from the Veteran Hospital in Tucson had said: remove the 70% blockage from the artery. After the previous study of my arteries at the Veterans Hospital in Wilmington, they told me that there was no justification for doing another at that time.

About two months after the ultrasound, my wife and I were at my son's house outside talking to each other. All of a sudden, my wife started to disappear. I could only see her from the shoulders up. I knew right away what was happening and remembered what that doctor at Southwestern Eye Clinic told me: "If it happens again, while you are not asleep, hold your breath and push as hard as you can, holding your breath to increase the blood pressure to push it through". I did what he had said at least five or six times. As soon as it went back to normal my wife drove me to the Veteran Hospital in Wilmington. They admitted me for the night and then I was sent to Christiana Hospital in Christiana, Delaware. Sometime in the evening I was talking to the nurse after she had given me my medicine, and just like before with my wife, the nurse disappeared from the bottom up and I knew what to do, so I was holding my breath and pushing as hard as I could. The nurse returned to her normal size.

After that, I called my wife, and she came to the hospital and stayed with me. My wife, the nurse and the doctor agreed that I should remain at Christiana Hospital and have a 70 % blockage removed from my left carotid artery. The doctor at Christiana Hospital said that because my right carotid artery was almost completely occluded, they had to make a bypass on my left carotid before they could operate. When I woke up after the operation, the nurse said they had quite a job keeping me alive; the operation had been a total success and several days later I went home.

I was told that the veteran's hospital was not very happy because I was only supposed to go to Christiana Hospital for an evaluation. I said to myself that if I had lost the vision on both sides, the first thing that came to mind was, *'Where is my 45 pistol?'* Obviously I had to see a psychiatrist. I said to him, "I just wanted to see if I needed to see you. The Veteran Hospital of Loch Raven was one of the worst veterans hospitals I had ever been in.

I remember a veteran who had a stomach ulcer. They tied him up in the wheelchair. He asked me to push the button to call the nurse several times because he needed to use the bathroom. I did call the nurse several times, but by the time someone showed up he already had his bowel movement on the chair. They took him with the wheelchair into the bathroom, and the nurse screamed at him like it was his fault. When they brought him back into the room, they put him into the bed and tied his hands and legs. After the nurses and the orderly left, I had asked him why they tied him to the bed. He said he was not sure, but maybe it was because of his drinking problem. He had a visitor who was introduced to me as his girlfriend. She was also concerned about him being tied up but she too didn't know the reason why. Late in the evening, three women tried to take blood from his arms and between his legs; it sounded like none of their attempts were successful. About 2 a.m. his bed was vibrating, and he was saying things that I could not understand. So, I called the nurse but she told me to go back to sleep. A few hours later a whole bunch of people came into the room and woke me up. I sat up on my bed to see what was going on; a man who saw me looking at them requested that I had to be removed from that room.

In the morning, a man came to ask me confidential information about the patient I shared the room with the previous day. It seemed strange: Why did he need to know who visited him and what other things I'd seen or heard. Then I asked about that veteran. The man told me that he died. I said that he probably died as a result of malpractice. Three nurses, trying to get blood from him collapsed all of his veins, perhaps at the cost of his life. Before leaving, he asked me what I would say if I had to testify. I answered that I would describe exactly what I had witnessed there: a patient treated like an animal - a tied up animal. I also told him that the veteran was still young and should not have died. I implied that they killed him.

It was the same Loch Raven Hospital, where 34 employees in the pharmacy had been arrested for drug dealing. A year later this veteran hospital was closed and a new one was built next to University Hospital in Baltimore.

I don't want to say that all veterans hospitals are bad. At the veteran's hospital in Tucson, Arizona, I was treated with respect and care.

15

How to Succeed in a Family Business

"I love those who can smile in trouble, who can gather strength from distress, and grow brave by reflection. 'Tis the business of little minds to shrink, but those whose heart is firm, and whose conscience approves their conduct, will pursue their principles unto death."

Leonardo da Vinci

We understood business as walking in the shoes of our clients and expecting them to come back with a wide-open smile, greeting us and asking for more. We never wanted to do anything thing that didn't include excellence. We always loved what we did. We worked not only with our minds, but with our hearts, as well. Ours was a family where love, respect, and humanitarian values were key. Extending this attitude towards the development of several family businesses came naturally.

Our business at that time was a family-owned corporation called Fueller's Investment, Inc. The five members of the corporation voted on whether to continue with the 70 room nursing home project. I was the president, and my younger son was vice president. We voted to continue with the nursing home, but my wife, my older son and my daughter voted against the idea.

The 23 acres had three homes and a construction building on it. At about the same time we also had two veterans' homes, Fueller's Septic Pumping Company; Fueller's Construction Remodeling; and, new home construction, as well. Buono Pizza Restaurant and I also became certified residential home inspectors.

During the time we had our family-owned businesses, my wife was also Mayor of Marydel, Maryland. For six years, my wife and I were working seven days a week, most of the time from 5 a.m. to 11 p.m. On weekends I would go out to potential customers and give out estimates for remodeling and making additions for homes.

We created Buona Pizza Restaurant. I made the pizza dough, starting at 3:00 in the morning. I let the pizza dough rise once , then cut it into a 20 ounce dough ball. The dough balls were put on a tray and later into the refrigerator for one more rise. I made 16 inches pizzas. Our pizza became very well known.

My youngest son was making pizzas and most of his customers were from the Fire Departments and the Air Force Base. The pilots from Dover Air Force Base would fly some of the pizzas to Andrews Air Force Base. There was a chef who was then, chef for President Ford; he worked at Andrews Air Force base and he relished the pizza that our younger son made. After enjoying it he said that it was "The best pizza that I have had in a long time". One Sunday afternoon, my wife and I were working at our pizza restaurant when this chef and his wife came to order a pizza. Before leaving our establishment they came and told us who they were and that they had hoped to see our youngest son, but Sunday was his day off. Our son was very happy to be praised by the president's chef. We were very proud of our pizza restaurant and of the dedication and hard work we put into it.

On Fridays and Saturdays evenings we had nine people working there. Our menu had cold and hot submarines, take-out dinners, hamburgers, hot dogs, buffalo wings, french fries and so many other tasty good quality food. Our customers always appreciated our meals and service.

The building we bought, used to house a liquor package store, but my wife and most of my family didn't like the idea of selling alcohol.

My son and I were taking out shelves and the old carpet to begin the remodeling. Curious people would stop by and ask what we planned to do in that building.

I said, "There is a clipboard and you can write down what you would like to have here in this building". Most of the people said 'a pizza place,' and that's how we decided to open a pizza restaurant.

There was a family from Italy that wanted to buy that package liquor store before we did. The reason the owner of that package liquor store did not sell the building to them was that the Italian man had approached the owner in a Mafia-type style. He decided not to sell it to them.

While we had our pizza restaurant we were very successful.

The head of the Italian family sent his people to verify that we really sold many pizzas. He called to see if he could buy our restaurant. I asked him, "Why would I sell the pizza restaurant when we were selling a lot of pizza?" But he insisted. He called several times and made me an offer. I said, "Every time you call I will raise the price $5,000". This went on for almost a year. At one point he asked what I would do if he sent someone in with a shotgun to hold me up. "I hope it would be you because if it is you, I will shove that shotgun up where the sun does not shine," I said.

My wife had a heart attack. Perhaps she had been working too many hours; perhaps the heart attack was my fault. My wife said she wanted $5,000 for the business name "Buona Pizza" which was her idea.

We finally sold our Buona Pizza restaurant to the Italian family, and my wife got her $5,000. We owned a minor subdivision about 3/4 mile from Marydel and I was clearing the land for a house lot. While bulldozing a tree, the top of the tree broke off and came crashing down, hitting the top of the hood and landing between my legs. I was pinned against the seat. I had to get a chainsaw to cut the top of the tree around where I was sitting. Again, an angel must have been there to protect me. The tree could have landed in my chest which would certainly have killed me.

At that same subdivision, I just set the poles for a 30 by 60 feet pole building on a wooded lot. It started to rain very hard and a bolt of lightning was moving closer and closer. I did not have enough time to get to my truck about 1/4 mile away from where I stood. A wooden pallet laying on the ground had the poles on it, and the water that was standing on top of the ground wasn't going anywhere. I thought, *"You'd better get off this wet ground since the water isn't going anywhere"*. I stepped on to the pallet when a few minutes later a bolt of lightning struck the oak tree. The oak tree was about 50 feet from where I stood. The crack from the lightning bolt was so loud that I could not hear for a while. I could feel the electricity running through my body. My hair was standing straight up and inside the bottom of my boots there was smoke. It truly ripped that oak tree in half. The angel that has been with me for so many years was there again.

In Henderson, Maryland I was installing a septic system where the owner of the house asked me to do it. Before digging with the backhoe I asked him where he wanted the septic system, and if there were any electrical wires, phone cable, or water lines where the septic system was supposed to go. He said that there were no electrical wires, phone cables, or water lines. On a normal septic system, I started from the house with a trench to where the 1,500-gallon septic tank goes, then the distribution box and the last four 50 foot lines (six feet between the lines), making a total of 200 feet referred to as 'the field.' As I was digging to where the tank was supposed to go, I grabbed a 240 volt electric cable with the digging bucket and it welded that electric wire to the digging bucket; 90 feet away it set the transformer on top of the electric pole ablaze. When a person is digging with the bucket, a front loader is usually pushed down in to the ground so the backhoe does not move. On the back end of the backhoe is a stabilizer which has bars that are set into the ground to stabilize the rig while someone is digging. And all of that was still connected to the ground when the digging bucket was shorted out by that 240 volt blast; the electricity flowed throughout the whole machine and through my entire body. I often wonder if they, the angels that protect me are always on alert; otherwise, I should have died so many times.

The electric company installed a new transformer and repaired the electric cable. The following day I dug the hole for a 1,500 gallon septic tank. A local septic tank builder brought the tank and placed it into the hole. Next came that distribution box and it was put into that hole approximately 6 feet from the septic tank. Then, I had to dig four lines each 50 feet long, starting with the first line on the outside. Digging about 20 feet along I ripped a four inch water line, and water shot up at least 50 feet into the air. Within minutes, the entire area was flooded; I look like I had just come out of a swimming pool with my clothes on. The four inch waterline fed the town of Henderson.

The owner of the house said that he did not know that there was a waterline running through his property, of course, that's what he said about that 240-volt electric cable. He did not know where the valve was to turn off the water that was submerging the whole area. His next door neighbor saw the water shooting up in the air and it also started flooding his property. He called someone to turn off the valve and they repaired that 4 inch waterline. I had to wait several days until the water was gone to finish the job. Thank God that no one got hurt on this job. Now there is an organization that goes out and looks for electric cables, water lines, sewer septic lines and so on and marks exactly where the lines where are.

My wife and I designed and built a Cape Cod house. We created three bedrooms, two bathrooms with this design in mind. We produced special boards made of Cedar and Ash, obtained from our farm in Minnesota. For the living room, the dining room wall, the living room floor, the dining room, bedrooms, and corridors, our number one preference was red oak. We were fascinated with the house we built on Cape Cod, but it was impossible for us to move there because our businesses demanded a lot of time. The house was left empty for three years until we finally decided to sell it.

Our youngest son Tony built his first home in our Fueller subdivision, on Fueller's Lane, and after he and his family lived there for some years, he sold it to a young man. In that subdivision there was a building that was 120' x 30' wide and at the top there was a bedroom, a living room, a dining room, a kitchen and a bathroom where I used to paint my paintings.

When our youngest son started building his second home, Tony and his family went to live there while he was building his second home. Tony is a craftsman of perfection. He does it all with great creativity and professionalism. I really can't think of anything he cannot do. I imagine our children were inspired to do excellent work from our example during all those years. I'm certain that all our dedication was a significant influence in the exemplary behavior of our children.

Tony and his wife were working for Fueller's Investment Inc. Tony was Vice President and his wife was Secretary and Treasurer. Then we found out that we would be able to re-submit an application for the nursing home and that it would take about three years for the construction to begin. At our next corporate meeting, we voted on whether to continue on with 70 room nursing home, and the majority once again ruled not to continue with the nursing home. My wife and I were thinking of slowing down and had asked Tony to take over our family-owned business, but he had no interest in running the business.

16

Oh, Love!

"The greatest happiness of life is the conviction that we are loved;
loved for ourselves, or rather, loved in spite of ourselves."

Victor Hugo

My wife had a heart attack, and we decided not long after this incident, in the Spring of 2000, that we should dissolve Fueller's Investment Inc.

We have always been passionate about traveling, exploring, discovering a world rich in adventures: something that my wife and I have always been very good at achieving together. Neither of us were afraid to immerse ourselves in adventurous journeys around the world and we adapted very easily to all the circumstances that appeared on our way.

One day, I read a very inspiring quote by Helen Keller that said "Life is either a daring adventure or nothing at all," and I strongly identified with this message. My heart was born to beat without frontiers, without labeling human beings according to their ethnicity or culture. Each person who lives on this planet is worthy of my respect and in some way can be my teacher. I have been fortunate that my wife, ever since the beginning of our relationship, wanted to explore the various cultures of the world with me. Throughout all our travels we have experienced all kinds of cultures: their customs, music, cuisine, and the pleasure of listening to exciting stories from the strangers who appeared along the way to entertain us and illuminate our trips.

Traveling through the world, accompanied by my great road companion, has been a blessing that I will treasure forever. I can assure you, that she, with her presence and love, has given me wings to go far and to overcome the most difficult moments in my life. My wife and I have created our love brick by brick, tear after tear, laughter after laughter: children, grandchildren, animals, homes, projects, and hardworking moments. I would never imagine, that the day of the rotten tomatoes would have taken us so far, in love, with so much impetus to overcome each obstacle on the way. But sometimes men deviate from their path at the siren's call of insistent temptation. We let ourselves be ignited by the flame of a transient, inconsequential passion that can burn and make ashes of the true love that has accompanied us in life. Yes, I admit that I have been weak, that I have let myself be carried away by a 'siren' song. I could not undo the damage this caused to my life partner, my marriage, my rotten tomato face. We decided to go back on the road and travel again.

We purchased a mini motor home and shipped it to Bremen Harbor in Germany. We visited our oldest son and his five children in the northern part of Germany. He is a Baptist Preacher, and he's been in Germany for twenty six years; he has his own church. We had a magnificent time there, enjoying the fruits of our marriage, surrounded by our son and his beloved family. We felt rewarded and nurtured by that visit.

After a while, it was time to hit the road again. We went to my wife's relatives in Heidelberg, to my relatives in Bruchsal, Germany, and on to Austria; then, we headed south towards Italy to explore Venice, Verona, Vicenza, and Milan. No one can ever have enough of Italy - we could have stayed there forever - but we decided to continue and went along the French Mediterranean coast, and from there to, Valencia, Spain. We planned on staying there for the Winter at a motor home park. My goal, once there, was to take art lessons at the University of Valencia, but the RV parks were closed for the winter.

We met a German couple on the way who told us that the closest place from there would be Benidorm — a place considered a mini-New York City. Benidorm was a magnificent seaside town to be on the eastern coast of Spain. Even its tiny fishing village was enchanted. It was a popular Mediterranean destination known for its nightlife. We walked holding hands over its sandy beaches regaled with palm-lined promenades, bars, and rows of skyscrapers. A nice mix of Caribbean paradise, with a hint of a world-class city. The place inspired my artistic spirit. I painted a few paintings. We stayed in Benidorm for about two months and met another couple who lived next to us in the RV park. He was a German medical doctor and a psychiatrist, and his wife was Italian. She was a school teacher.

I wished that the water was warmer; the doctor and his wife suggested that we accompany them to Fuengirola, a four hours drive. They pulled the trailer with their small car. I was amazed noticing at his treasure trove of books, piled high in the back of the trailer. I told him that he needed to put his books over the axle; otherwise he might lose control of his car. But, he insisted that he was fine. We left together and we followed him to Fuengirola. About five or six miles after we left, there was a downgrade of 5%. He was picking up speed and the trailer start to fishtail. I said to my wife, "If he hits the brakes too hard, he will lose control." Just as I finished telling that to my wife, he stepped on the brakes too hard and because the trailer didn't have brakes, the back end of the trailer slammed into the passenger side, where his wife was sitting. In the trucking business this was called a 'jackknife'. Thank God that his wife walked away with some bruises and no broken bones. With a furious tone she said in German, "Wann ich hatte ein messer ich trete ihm in schstikel freischneiden und tete gulasch von im machen," meaning "When I had a knife, I kicked him in a jumble and made goulash in the kitchen." I laughed and said, "Alana, just remember how much you love him." I understood her reaction. Despite all his learning, despite his knowledge of psychology, he was as stubborn as a bull.

My wife, and I went on to Fuengirola, Spain. The German doctor and his wife said that they would meet us there as soon as they fixed their trailer. They arrived about a week later and it was then that we knew that he had cancer. His favorite liqueur was Drambuie, a golden-colored liqueur made from a Scotch whisky blended with honey, herbs, and spices. Since he was not allowed to drink alcohol, he would buy me a bottle and I would have to take a sip and explain to him in detail how good it was. He didn't allow me to add ice. I had to drink it straight; I enjoyed the taste and enjoyed narrating my experience with this exquisite drink.

We travelled far and wide, exploring the wonders of nature, culture, and people, always ready to share with the open pages of their book of life. The European RV parks were more enjoyable than the American ones. We always found something to do; there was always some party to attend, people to meet, new experiences to get inspired by, and wine tasting fairs which were free of charge. European older adults are very energetic and are not waiting to die. On the contrary, every new day there is new hope and excellent reasons to keep on living an enjoyable life. I definitely share that mindset.

There was a bus stop not far from the RV park. We travelled by bus to different places on day trips. This was an easy and comfortable way to get to the small villages that were in the mountains and to the farm communities. We went to Granada, and saw Queen Isabel and King Fernando at the Cathedral. Granada was the place where the Moors ruled Spain for 1100 years. The Moors created wondrous buildings whose architecture is still fascinated today. The Moorish influence bequeathed an immense cultural richness to that region, nourished further by its rich traditions of dance, music, and culinary pleasures. The Moorish presence also accounted for the unrivalled beauty of the people. Their presence in Spain left a prominent mark that survived their expulsion by the Catholic monarchs, Isabel and Fernando, from that part of the country. We learned that the languages spoken in parts of the Iberian Peninsula under Muslim rule were Andalusian, Arabic, and Mozarabic. Long after the expulsion of the Moors, the Arabic influence on some Spanish words and expressions can still be heard.

My wife and I took a bus tour to where the black pigs roamed freely in the countryside, near the border of Portugal, an area with lots of oak trees bearing the fruit that these pigs were fed from. Spain is known for the most delicious and expensive hams, hams of many styles and great quality. We wanted to know more about their ancient techniques and we did.

In Spain and in Lisbon, Portugal, I was amazed by the way they cultivated their wine grapes. After harvesting the grapes, they cut all the grape vines back to the stump in preparation for the following year. I have tried wine from different regions of Portugal, and their tastes were delicious and different, because of the richness of the soil.

In Portugal, we wanted to visit Fatima. It is told that three children in Fatima 'received' the appearance of the Virgin Mary, who spoke to Lucia, the oldest of the three. This happened in May, 1917 and the Virgin presented herself as 'the Lady of the Rosary.' Several people prayed on their knees; I recalled having to kneel on that corn when the priest wanted to punish me. But these people lined up in attitudes of reverence did not feel pain in their knees. Their devotional act of faith and their belief that the Holy Mother would bless them and alleviate the sorrows transported them inwardly to a place of deep spiritual comfort.

We enjoyed travelling with our small motor-home. We could stop whenever we wanted to rest or to explore the region. This sense of freedom was deeply refreshing. Our only *agenda* was to 'go with the flow' and to enjoy wherever the road took us. In one of the parks we found a British couple who was selling their trailer at the RV park. We purchased it, but later we found out that the trailer could not stay there; nonetheless, we intended to go back to that RV park the following year. We put the trailer in storage.

We loved and enjoyed our eight-month sojourn in Europe. Those were very rewarding days. After months traveling as free birds, we delivered our motor home from Bremen to Baltimore Harbor in Maryland. Then we flew back to the United States. We traded that small motor-home for a larger one to continue our travels in the United States. The following year, we decided to go to return to Fuengirola where we had stored the trailer. We made other trips during our month-long stay in Spain.

It was about then when my wife's sister called. Their father wasn't doing well. My wife wanted to go home. We went to her parents' home and that Spring I returned to our home in Marydel. My wife decided to stay with her parents. She came to our house soon after to explain why she didn't want to come back with me. I suspected the reason, but she denied that it was because of what had happened between Carol and me. I knew from the very beginning seeing Carol was wrong. I knew it was wrong, but that didn't stop me from descending into the swampy ground of a clandestine affair. I wallowed in there, drowning all those beautiful years of marriage I had lived with my wife. I cannot undo the past, except remember that it has been left behind. I regret deeply that detour. Perhaps I was feeling lonely. Perhaps my ego wanted to have a different mirror to reflect a renewed image of my masculinity. I knew neither the source nor the cause of my betrayal. This is how it happened.

Every Summer I would go back to our farm in Minnesota to take care of the land. One of those years, Carol a friend we knew from the church, called me and said, "When I got off from work I drove by your place. I noticed that you were back on your farm, cutting up the brush." I was happy to hear from her and her family. That evening she invited me to accompany her, her brother-in-law, and his wife to a restaurant for dinner. They picked me up and after dinner took me back to the farm. The following day, after getting off from work she stopped by for a chat. I made coffee and she told me about her husband. He had been in jail for two years for stalking a woman (with whom he had an affair); he had two more years in prison. I was sorry to hear that; her husband was also a friend of ours. We had a nice evening talking about our families.

Another day she stopped by again. She invited me to a

restaurant later that evening. I realize now how naive I had been to see her so often. Listening to her stories about her husband, her family, our friendly conversation, only added fuel to the fire. I was an insect, walking on a spider's web. As soon as the opportunity arose, she began to smile in a certain insinuating way. I thought the possibility that she might be interested in me romantically was just my delusion. I felt somewhat uncomfortable with the very idea. But Carol became more direct and told me without preamble that she had a crush on me since we used to live there on the farm. And I thought to myself I also had crushes - but I soon got over them. I didn't know what to tell her and I left things hanging. I didn't want to take advantage of the opportunity. She felt that I was keeping her at a friendly distance. After that evening, she stopped in almost every day to chat. She frequently mentioned how much she missed her husband.

A few days later, she wanted to go to Target in Duluth, 156 miles from Ray. Ever the gentleman, I wanted to give her my friendly support despite the romantic insinuations. I didn't want to sacrifice the nice friendship we had built over the years. Hopefully her interest in approaching me would otherwise disappear; perhaps, it was the understandable reaction of a woman who missed her husband very much, a woman who felt very lonely. When we finished shopping, it was about 9 p.m.; it would take about three hours to get home, and it was the weekend. Carol was very persuasive about spending the night together, and I finally lost self-control. I surrendered to desire and after dinner, we spent the night in a hotel. Our Summer romance went on for a month. Something started to feel different and I became attached to her.

Winter was approaching. I told my wife that I was going to stay at the farm for a while to do some painting. I did some painting while Carol was working, but of course that was not the main reason I stayed. I was getting comfortable with Carol. She was using me. Then she asked me to leave her house. One evening after dinner, she said, "I think I might be pregnant." I felt my whole world falling apart, my marriage included. All of a sudden everything became clear to me. I was about to lose everything as a consequence of my weak behavior. I wasn't strong enough to prevent this relationship. My wife didn't deserve it, I didn't deserve it, and our marriage didn't deserve it.

It was then, when the veil started falling, that Carol said, "I called your wife and told her that we had sex." I went pale. I shuddered. At that moment Carol represented the death of everything I had always loved. She even seemed to relish telling my wife about our affair. "Why did you have to tell my wife about us?" I asked her. "I just wanted it to be over with us," she said. That was the end. Since that night I have never contacted her, and she has never contacted me.

My wife and I agreed we would separate while she was staying with her parents. We agreed that each of us was free to do whatever we wanted to, including seeing and being with whomever we want to be with. Without any legal advice from attorneys, we agreed to divide 50/50 everything we had in our possession. There was no fighting about who got what. We also agreed that we would help each other if and when dire circumstances arose. My wife will always be my wife. She will be my sweetheart forever. We have known each other ever since we threw those rotten tomatoes at each other. Wherever we go, we are always civil with one another. As long as I live she will be my wife, the mother of our children, the grandmother of our grandchildren and great-grandmother of our great-grandchildren. And I will love her until my very last breath.

17

My Time on Everybody's Island

"... miserable of all conditions in this world: that we may always find in it something to comfort ourselves from."

Daniel Defoe, Robinson Crusoe

After my wife and I separated, I returned to Fuengirola, a city on the Costa del Sol in southern Spain well known for its beaches. I saved the travel trailer in a German RV park about eight miles south of Fuengirola. It was the first time in many years that I was traveling without my wife.

In an RV park in Benidorm, Spain, I met up with the German psychiatrist and his wife. They were sorry to hear about our separation; I told them that I was sorrowful too but I learned that life is always a "way forward and never backward". It had been very cold and it rained a lot in Benidorm, so we decided to go together to the Canary Islands. There we could enjoy a good climate and swim every day in the Atlantic. I immediately put my trailer up for sale; I sold it the very same day. My German travel companions left their trailer in the park and we all went by plane to Fuerteventura, in the Canary Islands. From the plane, I could see how magnificent Fuerteventura was. I fell in love with the place immediately.

Fuerteventura, is one of the largest islands, after Tenerife, that belong to the Canaries. Politicians consider it part of Spain. It was declared a biosphere reserve by UNESCO; its capital is Puerto Rosario. I have always been interested in history and geopolitics. I consider this planet my home; boundaries disappear in the knowledge that each human living on Earth to me is my brother or sister. Continuing on to Fuerteventura and the pleasure of its climate was a good idea. The locals refer to Fuerteventura as 'the island of a constant spring.' I would call it 'Everybody's Island' since people from all over the world visit there - all kinds of fascinating and exotic people. Others come to start a new life, sometimes hiding from whatever they've done in their own countries.

We stayed in a hotel for two weeks. There I met a German real estate agent. He showed me a construction lot located towards the top of a mountain - the highest place on the island, 2050 meters high. The location was magnificent and had a fabulous view. I advanced 10% to buy a lot but a few days later, I was notified that the owner could not get a clear property deed and they returned my money. Then, the real estate agent took me to a bar and where I had a delicious soup made with goat meat. It was hard for me to believe that it was goat meat but then I found out that it had been seasoned with ingredients and spices from Morocco. It was the best goat meat I had ever eaten.

The landscape, the solitude, the beauty of the surroundings, inspired me to paint; I wanted to remember the land of the house that was at the foot of the mountain. I had a windmill on one side and on the other, the mountain. The number with which I registered the painting was 1000348. The painting was 18 by 24 inches.

I finally bought a good lot at the top of the mountain and contacted an engineer and architect to develop the whole project. He was in his sixties and also of German origin. The architect told me that he received his architect's degree in Argentina. We started to spend a lot of time together and he showed me many photos of him and his life in Argentina. As we went through the photos a strange episode occurred. "But this is Adolf Hitler, and she is Eva Braun," I said. "How is that possible? Are they alive and in Argentina?" "Yes!" he answered, then added, "And the child who is sitting in the water by Hitler is *me*. I am Hitler's nephew, and these two girls are the daughters of Hitler and Eva Braun . . ." I was surprised, stunned, and was worried, too.

We all heard rumors that Hitler did not die but that a double of his was murdered in his place. Hitler and Eva Braun escaped. But so many 'truths' were distortions in the final analysis, the truth could never be known. It is also possible that one of their daughters is Angela Merkel Chandler, now Prime Minister of Germany. I spoke with people who were in their eighties, in the Island of Fuerteventura, and they told me that they helped many Nazis escape - including Hitler and Eva Braun, who were brought secretly to Argentina and lived there under false names.

At the southern end of the island is a ship that was used in those years to secretly transfer the Nazi Germans who fled to Argentina. Now it is there, fallen and collapsed, forgotten like the many memories housed in its now silent interior. The building where the papers for the ghost journey to Argentina were organized sits on the southern part of the island.

At that time Hitler had been protected by the Spanish Civil Guard. I remember very well that when I was young, most

Germans never believed that Hitler and Eva committed suicide. Scientific investigations and DNA tests carried out in more recent times found that Hitler's remains were not the same as those recorded in his dental procedures. On the other hand, all this is denied by others who say the DNA proves that the remains are Hitler's. However, I have seen with my own eyes, in the photos that the German architect showed me, that the man whom he said was his uncle, the man holding him in his arms, was Hitler. The woman at his side was Eva Braun. My eyes could not lie and the man who showed me the photos did not lie either. Why would he lie? When I lived in Austria, at the age of 11, the front page headlines of Braunau am Inn newspaper said that Hitler would visit his mother.

Years later I wanted to buy an apartment and they showed me one of the bedrooms on the third floor, fully furnished, overlooking the ocean, mere steps from the beach. I had everything. All I needed to buy was a satellite system for television. The place belonged to a tourist complex, and had a swimming pool, a parking lot by the tennis court just in front of my apartment, a restaurant, a grocery store, and a bar. As I was also an Austrian citizen, I had no problem obtaining the residence documents for money orders that allowed me to buy a car and stay in Spain as long as I wanted.

After a while, the doctor and his wife returned to where they left their travel trailer and I continued to enjoy my stay. I thought of it as my very own paradise. I could walk from the apartment to the ocean on a paved path. There benches at 300 feet intervals and a bike path parallel to the walking path.

That path led to El Castillo by a street called Caleta de Fuste, near a tapas bar called Capitano. That's where I met a German man named Udo who lived in Spain for 36 years. Udo had married a Spanish woman when he lived in Valencia. His wife's parents were very wealthy, among the elite, and Udo, because of his poor family, was not accepted by his wife's family. Still, they were very much in love with each other. But, as his wife did not want to lose her inheritance, they decided to separate. He left Valencia for Fuerteventura and lived there as a tourist. For most of his life, he slept on the beach.

When I met Udo in Capitano, he was 52 years old, and he was very well informed about what was happening around the world. He spoke English, German and Spanish. He was a very sociable man and made friends easily. He could approach a person in a bar and make interesting conversation for hours while sharing a beer. It was thanks to Udo that I met many people who eventually became friends: Wolfgang from Austria, Maxi from Valencia, Marco from Italy, Bany and Susie from the United States, Ana from Austria, Helga from Germany, Maria from Bulgaria, Mada from Syndicat, Africa, and Christina from Colombia. This is how I was part of a group of multicultural friends from many parts of the world. We took turns hosting and met every Saturday. We spent Saturday morning until Sunday after midnight chatting, eating, drinking and sharing the expenses between us all.

When they invited me for that occasion, they asked me not to disagree with anyone's religious or political beliefs and not to speak ill of the country of any of the people who attended our meetings. It was magnificent. My heart had no borders and I could easily relate to such warm and open people from so many different cultures of the world. There was never a bitter experience between us and we respected the opinion of each and every person. However, some of the people among our group of friends were 'wanted' people in their countries. The government of Fuerteventura knew very well who these people were because it was their responsibility to report to the police from time to time. Anyway, as long as those 'wanted' people did not get into trouble they would never be deported. Occasionally, law enforcement from abroad tried to return them secretly to their country. But even Interpol have not been able to eliminate them. The Island depends mainly on tourism. The north end of the island has mostly British tourists, the southern end mostly German tourists — the most affluent people live on the extreme northern and southern ends of the island. In the central part of the island is a city called Puerto del Rosario, which is the capital of Fuerteventura and the cheapest place on the island. The apartment that I bought is located about 11 km from Puerto del Rosario.

If I had to choose, I would rather wear jeans than a tuxedo. but there were times when I had no choice but to dress elegantly in a tuxedo. On the other hand, I always felt more comfortable being with people who worked to live instead of spending time with the wealthy who do nothing but socialize and practice sports.

Fuerteventura is approximately 60 miles long and has more than two million goats that feed on the right side of the road. Everyone knew that I did not want to be disturbed between 9 a.m. until 4 p.m. since that was the time I dedicated to my paintings. It was a productive time; I painted 92 paintings in approximately two years.

Udo, Wolfgang, Maxi, Marco, and I met most of the mornings in my house or in a local cafeteria. They were my best friends. Udo lived 36 years in Spain; during some of those years he was married to his Spanish wife. He never returned to his home in Germany. His mother was already in her 80's and he was the only son but there were two sisters. On three occasions, one of his sisters and I gave him plane tickets to visit his mother before she died. Unfortunately, he sold the plane tickets each time and spent the money on beer. About three months before I returned to the United States, I had to take him to the hospital because his stomach had begun to ache heavily. He vomited blood. They did emergency surgery and they had to do blood transfusion too. The doctors told him he had to quit drinking alcohol and smoking because the next time he would not be so lucky. Unfortunately, not drinking for a month his addiction won out and he started again. On New Year's Eve, Udo said he would quit smoking. We made a bet: I would give him $5,000 if he did not smoke for a week. If he smoked before the end of the week, he would have to pay me $5,000. We shook hands on the agreement. On New Year's Day Udo, Wolfgang and I went to a restaurant for lunch. After lunch, Udo went to the bathroom and I told Wolfgang to go check because he was sure Udo would smoke. Indeed, Wolfgang found Udo smoking in the bathroom. As they returned, Udo was trying to convince Wolfgang not to tell me that he had been smoking. I told him that he did not have to pay me the money. The burden of his addiction was great enough and would soon take him to the grave. Not long after I returned to the United States, Wolfgang's brother Kerk called me and told me that Udo had died and that his wish was for his ashes to be dispersed in the Atlantic Ocean.

Wolfgang was a talented singer. Their families sang and played Austrian folk music and I enjoyed it a lot. He used to work as an independent electrician. And, he loved everything having to do with Native Americans. Everything from his clothes to his apartment had a Native American Indian flavor. He loved to dress and show himself off as a Native American. Sometimes he even brought his native American pipe to attract the attention of young women who thought he had a certain exotic and authentic air. He was such a character! When he was the lead singer of Austrian popular music, he was secretly married to two women and had children with both. When he turned 50 years old and applied for Social Security, one of his daughters arranged for him to travel to Social Security in Austria to sign some documents and then fly back to Fuerteventura. There was only one problem. Because he had not paid his child support for many years, the Austrian government had taken over and paid for the children. At his farewell party we asked him if there would be any problem with the Austrian Social Security Department. Wolfgang told us that the lady from the Department said that he could come in and then return to Spain. When his plane arrived in Vienna, the security people were waiting for him. But, just before leaving Fuerteventura, a doctor told him that he had a brain tumor. Wolfgang died shortly after returning to Austria. Perhaps it was fate that he his final resting peace was in his native country.

Maxi Colorado (Colorado was his surname) always wanted me to come to the United States to visit Colorado and the Colorado River. Maxi worked for a Spanish rooftop contractor. The parent company was located in Fuerteventura. Maxi worked for his boss in Fuerteventura and had been involved with his boss's wife while working in their home. When his boss discovered that Maxi was having sex with his wife, he sent him to work in Lansototo next to Fuerteventura, and we never heard from him again. When people asked what happened to Maxi, some responded that he had become food for the fish.

Marco was a bartender who had never written anything in his life. His sole achievement was to serve drinks from inside and outside the building. He had the uncanny ability to follow up on everything that people asked of him without ever making a mistake. Marco lived much longer than any of us on the island.

146

In his teens, he and two friends tried to rob a bank in Italy. He was the driver of the car and waited outside while his two friends robbed the bank. But, one day the security guard was killed and when Marco heard gunshots he escaped immediately. His two friends were caught and taken to jail. Marco decided to leave and hide in Fuerteventura.

The Police Department knew what he did in Italy but he also knew that since that tragic incident he did not cause any problems and dedicated himself to working hard; for that reason he was never deported. One day Marco brought a calendar of a city and asked me to paint that landscape for him. According to Italian tradition, when a Catholic Pope dies, all persons who have committed a crime are forgiven and acquitted of their sins. So when that happened, he went home to be with his parents and siblings and, after the visit, he returned.

One day I was enjoying myself just as God brought me to the world - without clothes. I was on a nude beach, lying on a lava wall about three feet high and drinking a beer. When I placed the glass down a small lizard, jumped into the glass and began to lick the beer with great enthusiasm. He did it again and again. On one occasion, a beautiful, sunny day, I was in the same place, minus the small lizard. Two young ladies were looking for a place to go. One of them asked if they could sit near me. They spoke German and I answered yes, of course. Those two naked women also drank beer and the little lizard promptly went to their glasses and licked their beer. It was something different! Being naked, making a barbecue, playing volleyball, playing soccer, lying on the beach: recreation as usual in Fuerteventura, no matter if you were old, young, underweight or overweight - everyone had fun being naked there. There were hundreds of places like the one I shared with that little lizard, but you had to get up early in

147

the morning to get one of those. It had been two years since Elisabeth and I separated. We communicated frequently by long distance, but it was not the same as seeing each other in person. I felt that the time had come to return to the United States. I had no problem selling my apartment; I sold it for what I paid for it. A couple - he was French and she was from Puerto Rico - bought the apartment. She had fallen in love with one of my paintings and wanted to pay for it but, instead, I gave it to her.

18

Honoring the Dreamer in Me

"If you're always trying to be normal,
you will never know how amazing you can be."

Maya Angelou

When I see myself from a distant perspective, it is hard for me to choose a proper label. Who am I? Perhaps some trait of inner freedom or a sense of spontaneity made it a natural for me to *'go with the flow'*. But which flow? The flow of inspiration? The flow of belief that the Creator will always lead me to the right path? The stream of a dreamer who becomes a doer?

During my childhood, I never thought that a lack of money was equivalent to being poor. I learned that being poor was a consequence of not having faith in God, not having a purpose, not even a dream. Being poor was not trusting the inner voice that it is always there guiding us through our unique paths in life. The lack of money had never been a problem for me. Money comes and goes and it should never defines our true selves at all.

I was lucky to have been born with this free spirit. What I

did all my life, was to encourage the dreamer in me to become the doer. My dreams propelled beyond barriers that others, more traditionally, more limited, might have considered 'the impossible'. 'Impossible'... I loved to transform this word so that it resonated inside my mind as 'in possible'. To play with the odds, to go the distance. To allow the Creator to manifest His Creation through me. And so I became a painter; an artist perhaps? Who knows. Perhaps a visionary, capable of building homes and businesses on an empty piece of land urging me to give it life. And I did all those things and gave life to them creating exciting new possibilities for the abandoned, practically invisible parcel of land.

Painting was a very special kind of flow, a journey with brushes and colors. Oh, I received so much peace and happiness immersed in my creative work.

My creative art production had been very prolific. I started an online art gallery to exhibit my paintings. My goal was to donate my earnings to the *displaced children* suffering around the world. It is estimated that over 32 million children have been displaced either as refugees seeking asylum, as a result of violence, conflict, all manner of abuses, and natural disasters. As I had been a 'displaced child' from a very early age, I knew about their suffering and about the danger that those children were exposed to.

A month passed since opening my online art gallery. Something was wrong. The art gallery to support the displaced children of the world, received very few orders. Someone in my family had ordered a printed painting; it was sent and this person received it, but the website didn't show any payment received. I immediately called the company that created the website and its billing account. explaining that I had sold one of my works of art

150

but the payment was not registered on the site's account. They investigated and discovered that the person who had created my website had also created another online account in the name of his wife (who was also an artist). They also had access to CD copies of the photos of my paintings. To make matters worse, I later discovered that I did not have control over the domain name of my website. It took a couple of months for us to solve that problem and to get the money from sales back to my account.

Sometime later, I was contacted by a person who needed to place a fence around a Country so that it would not influence another Country. Most of the money I was able to raise was donated to my eldest son who is a missionary working helping children in need. In the very near future, I will open another website. Its purpose will be to help the displaced children of the world who live in Alaska. But first I must finish the construction of my house in Arizona since there I would be during the Winter and in Alaska during the Summer. Both places will have a large garden where I can grow my own organic vegetables, fruit trees, and flowers as well. Three years after the surgery of the left artery of my neck, I was in Yuma, Arizona to spend the Winter in warmer weather. My wife and I were still separated. She was living in her parents' house, but then one day she called me to see if she could go back home to Marydel. I agreed that she could. I didn't ask her about her reasons for going back to the home in which we had once lived together. It was a nice feeling to know that I will return home in Marydel and she will be there living with me, together again. She had forgiven me for having been unfaithful. Sometime later I had cardiac bypass surgery. When I returned home, I had to walk slowly because of severe inflammation and severe pain in the knees. Between the pain in my chest and the pain in my knees, I asked God to let me die. If it had not been for my grandson, my mood would have completely collapsed. But, that child was a totally compassionate and generous being who in everything wanted to help both me and his grandmother, my wife. If it had not been for his angelic presence, I would have renounced this life. When he came to stay with us while his parents were working, he brought the Sun into our home. He gave us joy, motivating us to feel better every day. Perhaps the pain in my knees and chest disappeared because of the loving presence of my grandchild. Today he is 12 years old. All my ten grandchildren are precious to me, but this child's sacred love achieved was the best medicine I could ever have received.

My wife and I created a business together before my bypass surgery. We called it 'Marydel Statutory Pottery and More.' Many of the objects that we sold were created by our own hands and specifically, as decorations for courtyard gardens, and parks. We put the business in my wife's name and she was the designated seller of our products. As our business was seasonal, we were able to go to Arizona during the Winter months. We would normally close at the end of November and open the first week of April. I was creating some 160 different items and I worked most of the time on my own.

On one occasion I had created a three-level water source with the largest bowl weighing approximately 600 pounds. In order to remove the mold from the inner bowl I lifted the bowl with the front of the backhoe. After raising it with a backhoe to the height, I needed to get it out, I had to use a steel bar to remove the inner mold. I lowered it and when it was two feet off the ground, one of the straps broke and the bowl fell breaking it into pieces. If the strap had broken while I was standing beneath that container, it would have fallen on me and I would have been crushed and instantly killed. I praised God and once again wondered why He saved me from death so many times in my life.

Another time when God saved my life was when I was working on an extension ladder, installing a light on the ceiling. As I descended from the ladder thinking that I was on my last step towards the floor, I pulled the latter towards me and I went down. I must have been unconscious for over 40 minutes. When I woke up I had a big wound in the back of my head and there was blood all over the floor. A person who works alone is always at risk of losing his or her life if a severe accident occurs if no one is there to help them. God has always saved me. Maybe He would not let me die so I could tell the world what happened to the ethnic Germans in Yugoslavia.

The students of the schools, universities, and people of the world, have the right to know through their programs of education what happened to the ethnic Germans in the former Yugoslavia. They have a right to know about all the abuses of man vs man. Until now, writing my biography here in 2019, only a very small group know about it. The genocidal atrocities committed against ethnic Germans in former Yugoslavia are not taught in the schools of any country. There is still very little mention of those terrible massacres, so little as to amount to nothing. The major powers during that time, especially the former Soviet Union, Great Britain, and the United States have turned a blind eye toward these events. They knew what Tito did and they did nothing - or worse, they supported it. The reason why these great powers will not let the world know is that they, directly and indirectly, supported the terrorist dictator responsible for the genocide of ethnic Germans. His name was Josip Broz "Tito." He and the partisans, under his direct orders, carried out the genocide and were responsible for the holocaust of the ethnic Germans. Personally, I also know that after World War II ended, the massacres perpetrated by Tito continued full throttle against anyone who didn't follow his party and against the ethnic Germans. No government in power prevented those horrors suffered by innocent civilians.

I built rock gardens for the forest park. We had family picnics where we took our military veterans so they could have quality time in nature. Inside a rock garden, I carved a water fountain with a naked woman holding the spout in the center. It had an umbrella with water running over the umbrella to the concrete container. My wife occasionally organized a picnic for the church in the park and much to our surprise, some men went to the rock garden and touched the sculpture of the naked woman to bring them luck. Their wives were not happy seeing their husbands doing that. Some asked them why they touched the sculpture of the naked woman. I have observed that people in the United States have a totally different mindset compared with that of Europeans. Those who consider themselves very religious may feel that nudity is an impure act - even nudity in a sculpture or painting.

I used to paint nude women when I was in Europe. No one considered the body of a naked person as something obscene; the body was a part of life that could become a work of art (depending on the talent of the artist!). In my experience in Europe, neither men nor women are ashamed to exhibit their naked bodies, but here in the United States, it is taboo.

19

Growing Through Challenges

"That which does not kill us outright makes us stronger."

Friedrich Nietzsche

Elisabeth was in charge of our business 'Statutory Pottery of Marydel and More' for ten years while I was happy to let artistic inspirations flow and create more than 70 different pieces. My older brother was married to my wife's older sister. While we were busy with our Pottery business, they lived in Alaska. Once, they were going to Arizona for a wedding, and I had the idea of watching their place in Alaska while they were away. So that's what we did.

Arriving in Alaska, seeing all those beautiful mountains, reminded me of Austria. The air was much cleaner and people said that you could still make a great coffee directly from the water of the creeks in Alaska. I thought then of the pollution and contamination to which we were exposed in Maryland, and reports of the growing number of people with cancer. I fell in love with Alaska. When my wife and I returned to Maryland I carefully researched Alaska online. I wanted to know about their quality of life, what that state had to offer, and I also thought that it was the last frontier in the United States. I talked with my wife and we decided to invest in five acres that had fir trees. We were closing the ceramics business in Maryland anyway. The year after I bought the land, I went to Alaska to see it. I built a half circle path and cleared the area enough for the construction of the house and buildings. I was preparing the half circle path when my wife called me and told me there was a real estate person who wanted to list their Marydel business, and I needed to return to the house to sign the listing agreement with the real estate agency. Six days later I went back to Marydel to sign the documents necessary for listing our home and the business.

Two days later, my wife asked me to take her to the airport in Philadelphia to be with our daughter Tina (Santina). I know my wife well enough to know that when she made a decision, there was no chance of changing her mind. I took her to the airport. On the way, she told me that she had the right to decide what she wanted to do and that we both had the freedom to do what we liked. I always wanted my wife to be happy, so I supported her desire to being away from our marriage. We decided to separate without going through a divorce. She is the mother of our three children, the grandmother of our eleven grandchildren and, the great-grandmother of our four great-grandchildren plus another who is on the way.

During my time in Alaska, I traveled very often, driving my truck and the trailer. I savored the beautiful landscapes that our Creator had made for us on this planet. On the first trip, I drove through the lower part of Minnesota on Interstate 94 West. I was following a truck with an excavator on the trailer. Suddenly, I noticed one of the wheels flopping from side to side on the left side of the trailer. I thought that I better move away before the wheel came flying off. I had just moved to the left side when the wheel came off, bouncing on the road up to the height of my windshield - and right to my face. I stepped on the brakes so hard that my truck and trailer's tires were smoking. It missed my face only by a few inches away. Those wheels weigh about 200 pounds. If it had not killed me outright, it would surely have destroyed my face.

Before my first trip to Alaska, I drove to Arizona and picked up my motor home from the Yuma test field storage shed (at the Army station.) I tied the car to the motor home, and from there I went to Alaska. I enjoyed, and still enjoy, driving cross country. The spectacle of nature never ceases to amaze me.

It was early May - still very cold and with a lot of snow in British Columbia. I was driving through a mountain range at approximately 8,000 feet when there was a rock slide across the road. I did not have time to stop. The rocks were not large enough to damage the motor-home, but the axle on the car towing platform was not far from the ground. All the work I had to do to continue my drive took me over an hour — a freezing time under hard snow and extreme severe weather conditions. Later, I took all the tools from the toolbox and found a bolt. There was only one bolt, but it wasn't long enough to solve the problem. I feared I would never be able to repair the damage. But I finally did it, and all I can say is that this Guardian Angel was there again! That's how I managed to continue my trip to Alaska, driving through British Columbia, Canada and passing the Yukon territory of northwest Canada, which is magnificently wild and mountainous. Everything was so beautiful, with all kinds of animals: brown bears, mountain goats, sheep, timberwolves, elk with their babies, and fantastic bison (buffalo). What a sight, seeing especially hundreds of them lying on the road. I stopped and walked between them trying to get them out of the way, but they weren't going anywhere. The traffic had to recede and then the mountain police had to come and get the buffaloes off the road. Beautiful and very gentle animals: no fear of people.

Separating from my beloved wife was a harrowing experience. Nevertheless, we remained united by a great friendship. After so many years of marriage, after creating a great family, and all the houses and businesses, our union became like the relationship between two good siblings. We always knew how to support each other. Life is an adventure that deserves to be lived with great courage and with the confidence that at the end of the terrible journey, the hero would arrive at the goal, ready to begin a new journey of personal growth. We can inspire those who follow us on the path of life to not fear adversity. After all, adversity and its challenges are what make us better, stronger people.

20

Awakening Our Consciousness of Being Alive

"I will not let anyone walk through my mind with their dirty feet."

Mahatma Gandhi

My story begins from the time I was in my mother's womb and includes everything that followed since then. I am very grateful for all the opportunities I have had through the years to become a better person. I am also full of gratitude to the Divine Source that saved me from death so many times.

Since the decade I was born, in the forties, until the Twenty-First Century, I have seen a lot of evolution in technology, in the fields of science and medicine, and in the great efforts that many international humanitarian groups make to create and increase a global consciousness for the protection of our planet. The only thing that still causes me deep sorrow is to see, again, the growth of aberrant racist behaviors that are still being spread all over the world. I know that there is nothing I can do but express my anguish when I notice the continued development of racial hatred, growing globally instead of diminishing and bringing relief and peace to those who are most oppressed. I do not consider myself an activist. I am merely a human being who has suffered a lot as a result of discriminatory behaviors, and I would like to see a world where human beings treat each other with kindness, compassion, and respect. It makes me happy to see how humanity has progressed; as a result of our progress the lifespan has increased dramatically. In 1,900, life expectancy was about 45 years while in 2020 it will be over 80 years old.

Life. Not many people live with a full state of consciousness that they have been blessed with a perfect machine which, given sufficient food, water, and shelter, practically works on its own. It's like walking through life in a Formula-1 race car driven by one of the best pilots in the world: our brain. I have reflected at length about the processes of our conscious and unconscious mind and I have also wondered about those phenomena considered supernatural, or paranormal, some of them I have experienced myself.

When I consider my mind, I am amazed by all those things I know that I haven't learned academically or formally, yet, the knowledge has been always there, ready and waiting for me. Pondering this has led me to wonder about reincarnation or channelization of wisdom or knowledge from a Supreme Source.

I believe that my brain contains a great store house of knowledge about things that I have not learned during my life. This knowledge appears in my conscious mind when I need to use it. Does the Supreme Source govern and distribute everything from the realm of the collective unconscious? Or perhaps there are parallel worlds that coexist in multiple dimensions and sometimes 'a dimensional door' opens and information passes through, to the other side?

I've learned about 'the collective unconscious,' a term and concept created by Dr. Carl Jung. According to Jung, there is a part in our unconscious mind that taps into the common psychological inheritance of humanity. It is the instinctual aspect of our being. What if the 'collective unconscious' is our direct connection to the Highest Source to which we might all belong, eternally?

How about those 'wise' and inspiring insights that I have received throughout my life which rescued me from trouble? How about the angelic or the 'beyond this reality' beings that have come to save my life so many times? How should I understand those experiences? I know, there are some psychiatric labels to frame me and explain what the 'real' cause of those so called 'paranormal' activities and experiences were; but I have already proven that I have a healthy mind with a highly effective brain activity that always guides me through extraordinary experiences. I clearly sense when someone won't be a trustworthy person or when I am about to take a wrong turn. I've been in places where I clearly perceive the presence of someone living in another time and/or space. Yes, I am fully aware of these mental skills, and I am grateful that my consciousness is resilient enough to allow me to vividly experience paranormal dimensions and see what is in there for a 'window of time'.

Back to the Source of Knowledge, Wisdom, Love, and Healing powers. The paranormal, the unexplained, has and does occur many times in the most diverse cultures of the world. Like the experience of some highly evolved people who unconsciously 'tap' or 'plug' into the Source, and come up with some sort of invention or idea which happened to occur, almost simultaneously in another place - either close or halfway around the world. This also happens in a brainstorming session, when someone gets an idea, and another person says "I was just thinking about that!" These phenomena also include something that occurs every day, when a person is thinking of someone and at that very moment 'someone' calls. Telepathy? Plugging into the collective unconscious? Being open and receptive to what the Divine Source wants to tell us?

There are so many theories about the 'self' or the spirit that inhabits our body. Some speculate about the possibility of a 'walk-in'. The walk-in 'enters' just before the person passes completely and the body still has its vital signs. It uses part of the consciousness of the person who just left to continue its life with an enhanced spirit. It is believed that the original spirit is replaced by a more advanced one. The 'walk-in' gets into the body of the person about to die or in a coma state; it could happen when an intense traumatic moment is being experienced or as a consequence of a fatal accident. So, in the waking up process, the person still remembers the life of the original being while their 'new' tendencies and skills are progressing towards helping mankind.

These thoughts also keep me wondering about the 'what if?' What if I did die, or a part of me did all those times when I was so close to dying, and I received a walk-in spirit that came to improve the level of my original 'me'?

No matter which perspective I choose, I come up with only one conclusion: no one could have escaped from what almost killed me. Therefore, angels or walk-ins or the Divine Providence or the combination of all of these Superior Phenomena was there to bring me back to life time and time again.

The different religions and spiritual beliefs in the world refer to our Divine Source by many different names. Many religions think that they are better than the others or, even worse, they create a 'religious' basis to justify killing others in the name of their 'God'. I know we all have the same Creator to Whom we give different names, forms, colors, and prayers. I also know that the main Source of our Creator is pure love - love without condition or discrimination. It is a love full of compassion for all that is living, including animals and the natural resources that are all around us to bless our lives and the lives of our descendants. We all need to protect this miracle that we call 'life,' but too many of us take it for granted. Life is not for granted. We need to learn how to speak the language of love to anyone and everything that is living around us.

When governments and religious organizations say it is okay to kill others to protect the country or a religion, it is nothing more than a political and religious manipulation of the masses. Governments manipulate our minds by telling us that the war is happening for the best interest of all. Dark forces utilize a religious or a governmental scenario to play out the very worse for mankind. We just need to look back to see that this macabre negativity has been happening all over the world since the beginning of time. Very few have had the courage to speak the language of love. Unfortunately, that language is becoming more silent the more mankind continues on its involuted benighted journey.

I personally experienced hatred from my own platoon sergeant during basic training at Fort Dix, New Jersey. My platoon sergeant said that the only good thing a German is good for is to be used as a target when they need target practice. He had served in the Army during World War II, and after the war in Germany. He hated me just because I was of German descent. The Austrians hated me and my family when we lived there as refugees. Tito of Yugoslavia, executioner and master of genocide, along with his partisans hated everything that was German. Children raised under racist and sectarian beliefs inherited that hatred against anyone considered 'the other.'

Human beings often lack 'human' or 'humane' behavior because from childhood, we have been manipulated and taught to think and act inhumanely - in the name of God or in the name of a nation.

Before I leave this world definitively (or temporarily!), I would like to see people 'wake up' from the hypnotic force that has turned them into puppets of governments and religions. I would like to see more compassion: more compassion in a world where no intentional harm to anyone or anything is living the planet is the norm. I would like the mental and spiritual fog to dissolve so that the Divine spark that ignites each one of us can shine its merciful and compassionate light on every human, animal, and plant that lives on our planet. Wherever the world is headed right now, led by the powers that rule the Earth, doesn't seem like a particularly good destination for our planet.

I heard once that the Dalai Lama said, "If you can, help others; if you cannot do that, at least do not hurt them."

I would like to close this chapter with a quote from Martin Luther King, Jr.:

"The most urgent and persistent question in life is: 'What are you doing for Others?'"

Many wise and compassionate souls have walked our planet trying to inspire in all of us the sublime idea of awakening our highest state of consciousness to provide the best for ourselves, our families, and for the rest of the world.

It would be a blessing if the love of those higher beings hasn't been in vain, and if it is not too late, to expand their great purpose throughout the world.

The End

Made in the USA
Middletown, DE
09 August 2022

70955090R00106